I0139448

Bridge for Peace

Foundation for Healing

Annette M. Eckart

Bridge for Peace Publishers
Wading River, New York

Bridge for Peace Publishers
PO Box 789
Wading River, NY 11792

First Printing, January 2011
Second Printing July 2017

Foundation for Healing
Copyright © 2010 by Annette M. Eckart

ISBN 978-0-9845306-0-1

For use with DVD *Foundation for Healing* © 2005 by Annette Eckart
Available through Bridge for Peace, PO Box 789, Wading River, NY 11792
Phone (631) 730-3982 fax (631) 730-3995
www.bridgeforpeace.org

All rights reserved.
No part of this publication may be reproduced or transmitted in any form or by any means, electronic or mechanical, including photocopying, recording, or any information storage or retrieval system, without prior permission in writing from the publisher.

Scriptures in this book include direct quotations, as well as the author's adaptations, from various translations of the Holy Bible.

Printed in the U. S. A.

TABLE OF CONTENTS

INTRODUCTION

Isaiah 53:1 asks, "Who will believe our message?" The prophet continues by foretelling the coming and passion of Jesus Christ. Isaiah said, "…He was pierced for our transgressions, He was crushed for our iniquities; the punishment that brought us peace was upon Him, and by His wounds we are healed." (v.5)

The message of Jesus Christ becoming our substitute, bearing our punishment for sin, and gifting us with peace, still challenges us. Some will find this course confrontational, but God enforces His Word and demonstrates His power *today*. God has healed thousands, including paralyzed, deaf, blind, and speechless people, through Bridge for Peace worldwide. I have placed my hands on sick people and felt lumps and goiters dematerialize through the Blood of Jesus Christ. I have prayed with cancer and tuberculosis patients and they have been healed through Jesus Christ. This is a firsthand account of Jesus Christ's extraordinary work worldwide through committed Christians in Bridge for Peace.

I pray the Holy Spirit will instruct, empower, and equip you. I hope this course will not merely add to your knowledge, but that it will increase your passion for Christ and release you into a salvation, healing, and deliverance ministry to hopeless and suffering people. If you already pray for people and witness healings, I pray the scripture studies and testimonies to His might will strengthen and encourage you to persevere. "…the punishment that brought us peace was upon Him." Jesus is our Bridge for Peace.

Annette M. Eckart

Suggestions on How to Use this Course

Individuals have tested the *Foundation for Healing Course* in New York, and Patti Gordon of Bridge for Peace led a home group through the course. Based on their feedback, I have edited the course, adding support scripture and examples for clarity. Participants reported life-changing revelations as they went through the course. Some of the following suggestions on how to optimize your study come from their experience.

I strongly suggest you view the DVD with the Course book. View the first twenty minute teaching, then begin the corresponding lesson. The DVD is *my* experience, the Course workbook is *yours*. I recorded the DVD to help you learn from my twenty years of listening to the Lord, studying His Word, and praying for people worldwide alongside my husband Ed and with Bridge for Peace teams. Throughout the years, God sent people to help us— special thanks to the Chapmans and the Colebrooks. If you prefer, the course *can* be used without the DVD.

This material can be used either as an independent study or with a group. There is space to record your notes, so you will not need a separate notebook. You will need the Bible(s) of your choice. If you plan to study alone, the course is divided into twelve sections. Again, I recommend you view the DVD, then delve into the accompanying lesson, working at your own pace.

Ideally, if you plan to lead the course as a group, plan fourteen meetings. Patti Gordon gave her group participants a schedule. Overall, they met weekly, but sometimes a break was scheduled due to holidays. The itinerary kept everyone informed of what would be covered and was a handy reference to check the meeting dates.

Patti had several participants who had never met each other, so she began with a getting-to-know-you dinner in her home. She distributed the Course Workbook at that meeting. At the end of the evening, the group viewed DVD Lesson One. During the week, the participants completed Lesson One. The next week, they discussed the questions. At the end of the evening, they viewed Lesson Two.

If you are doing a group study, I suggest you split Part Two Lesson Four "The Blood Covenant Prayer" into two weeks. The material is too rich to be covered in one session. To divide the lesson, cover Blood Covenant Prayer: Examining the Prayer, Power for Healing and Power for Equipping, pages 61-65 in one week. The following week, cover the next segment of the Blood Covenant Prayer: Power for Repentance, Power for Forgiveness and Power through Prayer, pages 66-71. If you split the lessons, you will total fourteen sessions. On the last meeting, evaluation forms were distributed.

God bless you as you undertake the *Foundation for Healing Course*. Enjoy your exploration of God's Word. Ponder the questions; take time to search your heart before responding. Invite the Holy Spirit, our Perfect Teacher, to guide your study. I am sure God will give you new and exciting understandings.

Foundation for Healing

<u>Part One</u>

PART ONE

LESSON ONE

COVENANT

Why is covenant important to you? We find our place in the story of thousands of years of recorded history by studying covenant. Read, study, turn pages of scripture, and a pattern emerges. Men and women enter into divine covenant, falter, and discover God's faithfulness. Find hope in examples of covenant-keepers who, though repeatedly pounded under the hammer of oppression, remain faithful. Celebrate God-given grace triumphant within them, while grueling conditions surrounded them. Realize God's victorious power can characterize your life today. Reexamine personal failures and successes against the backdrop of centuries of human nature. Newly appreciate who God is and who we are in this moment of time, reawaken to the battle of spirit and flesh. God's relentless, extravagant love amazes us as we focus on covenant. We write a new chapter of history. God intends *you* to be a hero of faith. Accept His offer to covenant with Him or reaffirm your commitment. Your choice will yield results as different as a blessing is from a curse, as different as life is from death.

COVENANT

My husband Ed and I explored the possibility of purchasing land. The previous owners had made an agreement with the town called a covenant. Both town and landowners hired lawyers to represent them in establishing a covenant. Through the covenant, the parties agreed to restrict the land's use to certain activities. Our lawyer advised, "This covenant can never be removed." The town and future owners were both legally bound by the covenant's terms.

God has initiated binding covenants, or agreements, with humankind throughout history including Noah, Abraham, and Moses. Essentially, God said, "I will do this if you will do that." God selected men to perform sacrifices to seal His covenant agreements that affected future generations. They became mediators of the covenants. As we will see, covenants require action from two parties. Action is required of those who choose to enter a covenant with God.

> **We enter into covenant with God when we choose to serve Christ.**

NOAH

1) God made a covenant with Noah. (Read Genesis 8:20-22.)
What did Noah do?

_____

_____

2) What did God do?

_____

_____

ABRAHAM

God made a covenant with Abraham (called Abram at the time, God later changed his name to Abraham). (Read Genesis Chapter15.)

3) What did Abraham do? (v.10)

_____

_____

4) What did God do? (v. 18)

_____

_____

_____

_____

5) Can you share a personal experience of covenant including the action required of both parties?

_____

_____

From the above study we see how two parties are bound by covenant. The word covenant is easily defined by the dictionary, but not easily planted in our hearts. God is faithful to His covenant. He is true to Himself. God has no problem with self-control, boundaries, compulsions, self-discipline, impetuosity or unrestrained passions. God is not like us. We can know what a covenant is, but still not know how to keep covenant with a Holy God.

We sometimes convince ourselves the end justifies the means. God *is* justice. One day He will judge the nations. We excuse our guilt and employ relative thinking. *My sins aren't bad compared to someone like Hitler. After all, I'm a good person on the whole.* Jesus counters our relative thinking in Matthew 5:27. He says when we look lustfully at someone we commit adultery. How many people drool over movie stars, male and female, without a pang of conscience? How many people find it absolutely acceptable to lust after musicians and television personalities?

Knowing what the Lord requires of us that we might have eternal life does not necessarily cause us to change. In Australia, a straightforward warning is emblazoned across the front of Australian cigarette packages, "SMOKING KILLS". People read the message, "smoking kills", but don't necessarily change their smoking habits. We may realize there are consequences to ignoring God's warnings, but stubbornly refuse to "limit" our freedoms by obeying God. Indulging ungodly impulses under the delusion that these behaviors will bring happiness deepens bondage, skews discernment, and leads to death. We wrongly view God as a dictator. What seems limiting to our fallen nature is ultimately freeing. If we obey God's covenant we can rely on God to fulfill His life-giving promises. God's power backs His Word, as demonstrated in Abraham's story.

God reaffirmed His covenant when Abram was 99 years old. (Read Genesis 17:3-27.)

6) What did God ask Abraham to do as a sign of the covenant agreement between God, Abraham, and Abraham's descendants?

_____

Abraham's circumcision, a permanent mark cut into his body, was a permanent sign of the covenant God made with Abraham. would remind Abraham of God's covenant promises.

7) God's promises to Abraham: (Read Genesis17:3-8, 19.)

a)_____

b)_____

c)_____

In old age, Abraham and Sarah conceived their son Isaac. Abraham was born in 2166 B.C. Isaac was born in 2066 B.C. Then God confirmed His covenant again.

8) What did God ask Abraham to do? (Read Genesis 22:1-18.)

_____

_____

9) What did Abraham do?

_____

_____

10) What did God do?

_____

_____

11) What did God say?

_____

_____

MOSES

Over 500 years later, God made promises to Moses. (Read Exodus 3.)

12) If Moses would return to Egypt, God promised to rescue the Israelites from

_____ and lead them to _____(v.16-17)

God called Moses up Mt. Sinai to propose a covenant. (Read Exodus 19:3-8.)

13) What did God want the Israelites to do?

_____

14) What did God promise the Israelites if they agreed to the covenant?

_____

_____

15) How did the Israelites respond?

_____

God detailed the Israelites' responsibilities in what has come to be known as the Ten Commandments, ten famous covenant rules. (Read Exodus 20:3-17.)

16) What are the Ten Commandments?

1) _____

2) _____

3) _____

4) _____

5) _____

6) _____

7) _____

8) _____

9) _____

10) _____

God taught Moses and gave him regulations. Moses explained these to the Israelites. The people agreed to obey them. Moses wrote down God's teachings and regulations and built an altar. (Read Exodus 24:1-8.)

17) What action did Moses take in word and deed? (v.1-7)

a) _____

b) _____

c) _____

d) _____

e) _____

f) _____

18) How did the people respond?

_____

19) Then what did Moses do? (v.8)

_____

20) What is your understanding of a covenant?

_____

_____

Moses teaches the people about the importance of blood. He prepares us to understand the purpose of the blood in healing ministry today.

21) What did Moses say about the blood and the covenant?

_____

_____

Moses spoke to the Israelites on God's behalf as a mediator. He stood between God and the Israelites. He ordered the sacrifice and sprinkled the blood that confirmed that God had made an agreement with them called the Old Covenant.

22) What is the role of a mediator?

_____

_____

23) Have you had any experience with mediation or do you know anyone who has? Under what circumstances was a mediator sought? What happened?

_____

_____

ADAM and EVE

Let's go back to Paradise, the beginning, and apply our understandings of covenant and mediator.

Adam and Eve sinned by disobeying God in the Garden of Eden. (Read Genesis 3: 1-24.)

God banished them from the Garden of Eden. We were not in the garden when Adam and Eve disobeyed God. Why don't we get a chance to live in Paradise?

24) Read and paraphrase Romans 3:23.

_____

_____

The Bible says Jesus came into the world to save sinners. (Read 1Timothy 1:15.) That's good news!

25) Have you ever sinned—lied, envied, stolen, used God's name in vain?

_____

Our sinfulness shows how we, like Adam and Eve, disobey God. The Israelites promised to obey the Ten Commandments and could not. We cannot keep the Ten Commandments. The Ten Commandments convict us of our sinfulness. We need a New Covenant because our own actions damn us. (Read Romans 3:20.)

God promised in the Old Testament to make a New Covenant with us. The covenant God established with us through His Son Jesus Christ remains today. As in other covenants we've studied, action is required of two parties. If we enter into covenant with God, we choose to serve Jesus Christ.

> "...for through the law comes the knowledge of sin."
> Romans 3:20

26) What does God promise in the New Covenant? (Read Hebrews 8:10-12.)

_____

_____

_____

_____

27) Who mediated the New Covenant? (Read 1Timothy 2:5-6.)

_____

28) What did the New Covenant Mediator do?

_____

_____

Marriage is a covenant. Marriage is a legal agreement between two people who are attracted to each other, choose to leave behind their former lives to enter a permanent relationship, and embrace new life together. They make a public commitment to each other, promise to love each other, to become the priority in each other's lives, and are united through a new intimacy.

29) How is the New Covenant similar to marriage?

_____

_____

_____

_____

30) What are some differences between the Old and New Covenants?
(Read Hebrews. 10:16.)

Old Covenant	New Covenant
Based on law	Based on _____
Written on stone	Written on _____
Mediated by Moses	Mediated by _____
Taught by Moses	Taught by _____

31) In your own words, describe the New Covenant.

_____

_____

32) What is required of you to enter God's New Covenant? Personal answer.

_____

_____

Committed couples listen to one another and deepen their relationship.

33) How do we grow in our New Covenant relationship with God?

_____

_____

PART ONE

LESSON TWO

THE BLOOD COVENANT

John Immel, retired police officer, suffered with debilitating knee pain. The doctor advised knee-replacement surgery. Ed prayed for John through the power of the Blood of Jesus Christ. John's knee replacement surgery was cancelled! People ask, "Why do you pray, 'The Blood of Jesus'?" In this section, we begin to explore the significance of Christ's Blood. Many associate "blood" with traumatic and negative experiences and feel repulsed by the thought of it. If you are revolted by blood, ask the Holy Spirit to heal your fears. Phrases like "The Blood of Jesus" or "The Blood of the Cross" are life-statements. Our salvation depends on the Blood of Jesus, as does our healing, our deliverance, and our provision. As we explore the biblical significance of blood, ask the Holy Spirit to impart supernatural understanding about Jesus Christ's sacred Blood.

> **People ask, "Why do you pray, 'The Blood of Jesus'?" In this section, we begin to explore the significance of Christ's Blood.**

ADAM and EVE
(Read Genesis 3.)

God gave Adam and Eve dominion over all the earth (Genesis 1:26). They chose disobedience and forfeited dominion. Adam and Eve lost their innocence, saw their nakedness, and felt ashamed (Genesis 3:7). They made coverings for themselves to hide their nakedness.

1) Adam and Eve made a covering of

_____

2) God knew the inadequacy of the man-made covering and provided Adam and Eve a covering of

_____ (Genesis 3:21)

3) What had to happen for God to make an animal skin covering for Adam and Eve?

_____

The shedding of blood was necessary for Adam and Eve's covering. This was the first blood sacrifice.

ABRAHAM
(Read Genesis 15:1-21.)

As we begin chapter fifteen, we remember aged Abraham (then named Abram) was childless, his wife Sarah (then Sarai) was beyond childbearing years. God restates His promise to Abraham of descendants and a new land. God orders a blood sacrifice so Abraham would understand God was serious about His word. Abraham understood, as any man of his generation would, the sacrifice "sealed" God's promise to provide Abraham with descendants too numerous to count and a new land.

Webster's definition of covenant is: "a binding or solemn agreement made by two or more individuals to do or keep from doing a specified thing."

The biblical word covenant means "*cut*" in Hebrew, referring to the ritual of walking between rows of *cut* flesh pieces. Today, people "cut" a deal. The ritual Abraham performed in Genesis shows the origin of covenant implied blood sacrifice. We are privileged to observe this solemn meeting between God and Abraham through scripture.

Enter into the passage as you read. Imagine Abraham bent, slashing the heifer's flesh, wrestling with the knife, the smell of blood, Abraham huffing under the weight of the body, positioning it with bloodied hands. Visualize Abraham flailing his arms at vultures, guarding the sacrifice. What happened as, exhausted, he slept? What was it like to feel the horror and great darkness? How might God's voice sound? How might Abraham have felt when he heard God's words? Picture the eerie atmosphere of flame and smell the smoke. Through the ritual, God seared the promise of His faithfulness into Abraham's mind forever.

4) What animals did God tell Abraham to assemble?

_____

5) What did Abraham do with the animals?

_____

_____

6) God clearly specified what he desired as a sacrifice. Have you ever heard God ask you for a specific sacrifice? What was your experience?

_____

_____

7) Abraham fell into a deep sleep, saw a terrifying vision, and heard God's promises again. Do you remember a time, perhaps a frightening time, or an instance when you needed reassurance, when God confirmed His promise to you?

_____

_____

Fire and smoke symbolize God's Presence, His holiness, and zeal.

8) How did God participate in the ritual of sealing a covenant with Abraham?

_____

God spoke the language of Abraham's culture. By initiating this ceremony, God communicated the seriousness of His promise to Abraham. In Abraham's world, this blood sacrifice ritual sealed a solemn covenant between two men. In their civilization the ceremony meant, "May I be destroyed like these animals if I fail to keep my promise to you." Breaking the covenant had the gravest consequences. Abraham knew God established a covenant with him through the blood of the animals.

> **God spoke the language of Abraham's culture.**

9) God used the language of the day to communicate His promise to Abraham. What are some ways God communicates with *you* today?

_____

_____

God miraculously fulfilled His promises. (Read Genesis 21:1-7.) Abraham and Sarah conceived Isaac in old age.

10) Do you remember the joy of a long-awaited promise fulfilled? Explain.

_____

_____

Isaac was the fulfillment of God's promise. (Read Genesis 21:12.)

11) What did God say would happen through Isaac?

_____

_____

After fulfilling His promise, God grabs our attention with a startling command. God asks Abraham to sacrifice Isaac. (Read Genesis 22:1-2.)

We are shocked and wonder, *why would God ask for Isaac's sacrifice*? Idol-worshippers sacrificed children (Leviticus 18:21), but how could our loving God request Isaac's slaughter? A crucial scene in salvation history unfolds as father and son climb Mount Moriah. (Read Genesis 22:3-18.) God's purposeful acts press toward restoration.

12) Abraham instructed Isaac to carry the wood. He was to be sacrificed on that wood. How do you feel about that sacrifice?

_____

_____

13) Jesus agreed to carry the wood. He was to be sacrificed on that wood. Whatever your feelings about Abraham's sacrifice how do they compare with your feelings about our Father God's sacrifice?

_____

_____

_____

_____

14) What does Isaac ask Abraham? (Read Genesis 22:7-8.)

_____

15) What does Abraham reply?

_____

Abraham's reply prophesies the death of God's only son Jesus Christ as the perfect sacrificial lamb.

16) What did Abraham see? (Read John 8:56.)

_____

_____

17) We can feel pain and joy at the same time. Have you been able to see into the promised future as Abraham did while in the midst of a painful circumstance?

_____

_____

_____

Abraham built an altar, prepared wood to burn the sacrifice, tied Isaac, and placed him on the altar. Abraham raised the knife to kill his son as a blood sacrifice. (Read Genesis 22:9-13.)

18) What did God's angel do?

_____

19) What does God say?

_____

_____

_____

20) What does Abraham sacrifice?

_____

Isaac does not die; the ram becomes a substitute burnt offering. (Read Romans 5:6-11.)

21) Romans 5 tells us that Jesus died for _____. The ram substituted for Isaac. Jesus became our substitute. Jesus substituted His _____ for ours.

The Bible says we have been made right in God's sight by the Blood of Jesus Christ. Jesus took our sin penalty. (Read Romans 6:23.)

22) What is God's penalty for sin?

_____

23) How are we freed from the death penalty?

_____

Abraham tells his servants to wait with the donkey while he goes on with Isaac to worship. (Reread Genesis 22:5.)

24) Who does Abraham say will return?

_____

25) As scripture shows, Abraham fully intended to kill Isaac. What could Abraham's reply mean? (Read Hebrews 11:17-19.)

_____

As previously stated, what seems limiting to our fallen nature is ultimately freeing. Abraham chose to obey God, submitting to God's will. God did not force Abraham to obey. If Abraham refused God, he would not have seen the blessing. God was still able to bless Abraham, but will not violate His covenant. Our God limits His omnipotence because He wants us to freely covenant with Him and love Him.

Paradise was meant for a pure people. Adam and Eve chose sin. God could not allow them to stay. They freely chose to live under satan's rule. As stated in the previous lesson, God has no boundary problems when He establishes a covenant. He does not act impetuously. God urges us in Deuteronomy 30:15-20 to choose life, to choose whom we will serve. God gave us free will. At the same moment, He chose to limit Himself. Scripture clearly outlines several ways God has chosen to limit Himself.

Psalm 78 recalls how people "limited the Holy One of Israel." God wanted to bring them into a new land, but was limited by their disobedience.

Matthew 23:37 shows us how Jesus longed to closely guard and nurture people, but could not because they "would not." Jesus was limited by the people's response.

Mark 1:45 records how Jesus could not go openly into town. The healed leper's misplaced enthusiasm (disobedience) forced Jesus to avoid towns, limited Him in the towns He could visit.

Mark 6:5 tells us how lack of faith limited Jesus Christ's ministry.

Malachi 3:10 details how God was limited, because the people did not give. He could not bless them, when His nature is to bless.

Covenants require action of both involved parties. If they would not, God could not. God is limited not because He is weak, but because He is faithful. God is looking for the obedient in order to do marvelous things. God used Abraham to set a legal precedent that would free us from satan's power.

26) Who is the god of this world? (Read 2Corinthians 4:4.)

_____

27) Whose power is this world under? (Read 1John 5:19.)

_____

28) Where does satan reign and where does he work? (Read Ephesians 2:2.)

_____

Whenever satan is mentioned, we can expect strong reactions. Some people say satan doesn't exist. Others find him everywhere. The previous scriptures tell us the truth. Satan is alive and he is limited.

Adam and Eve chose to disobey God; they were cast out, cursed, and would endure physical death. Their sinful choice subjected them to satan's evil power. They chose to believe satan, broke God's law, and became subject to the legal consequence of sin. God longed to restore humanity through a New Covenant ratified with blood. God made covenants with Noah, Abraham, Moses and others, sealed with animal blood. These covenants could not free sinful humanity from satan's dominion. Yet, the time of the Perfect One, Jesus Christ, drew near.

Jesus, speaking of His death, said the time of judgment for the world had come.

29) Who did Jesus say would be cast out? (Read John12:31.)

_____

30) How do you feel about the reality of satan as the Bible describes him?

_____

_____

_____

_____

_____

_____

MOSES

God established a system of blood sacrifice for the forgiveness of Israel's sin. (Read Hebrews 9:1-6.)

31) What were the two rooms called in the tent of meeting?

_____

32) How were the two rooms separated?

_____

33) What was in the first room?

_____

34) What was in the second room?

_____

_____

35) What did the Ark of the Covenant contain?

_____

_____

The Ark had a pure gold lid—the atonement cover. Two hammered gold angels with spread wings were attached to the atonement cover making it one piece. The angels faced each other and looked down on the atonement cover as though hovering over it.

36) Why was the Ark of the Covenant or Ark of the Testimony important?
(Read Exodus 25:22.)

_____

_____

Moses received specific instructions for blood sacrifice. A man laid hands on the head of an animal to symbolize identification with the animal as his substitute. He symbolically transferred his sins to the animal (Read Leviticus 1:1-5.) The man brought the animal offering, laid hands on its head, and God accepted the offering as the sinner's substitute.

37) What is your understanding of this system of substitution?

_____

_____

_____

Man brought both his sacrifice and his repentance to God. This system of worship was a limited, temporary arrangement. (Read Hebrews 9:9-10.)

38) What was the limitation of this Old Covenant system?

_____

Moses received strict rules regarding worship. (Read Hebrews 9:7-8.)
Only the high priest was permitted once a year to enter the Holy of Holies, or the Most Holy Place. His entrance was conditional.

39) On what condition could the high priest enter the Holy of Holies?

_____

40) What was the blood's purpose?

_____

41) God could only be approached with_____

JESUS CHRIST

A New Covenant was established by Jesus Christ's blood. (Read Colossians 1:13-14.)

42) What has Jesus Christ done through His blood sacrifice?

_____

_____

The Old Covenant could never obtain forgiveness of sins for us. (Read Hebrews 9:11-18.) Let us intentionally explore the two covenants with the hope of increasing our understanding of the old foreshadowing the new and perfect covenant.

43) On an annual basis a high priest would enter the Holy of Holies. There were a succession of high priests assigned this privilege. Who is High Priest forever?

_____

44) The high priest entered the temple sanctuary. What sanctuary has Jesus Christ entered?

_____

45) What happened in the temple when Jesus Christ died? (Read Matthew 27:50-51.)

_____

Jesus Christ's shed blood tore the temple curtain that separated the Holy of Holies from the Most Holy Place. The torn veil symbolized the destruction of the old system of priests, giving us access to God through the Blood of Jesus Christ. The temple system on earth was a copy of the things in heaven. (Read Hebrews 9:23-28.) Under the Old Covenant the high priest could enter the Holy of Holies only with blood of animals, only once a year. An annual atonement for sin was necessary. An animal substituted for the people, taking their sins.

46) How is the annual atonement ceremony performed by an Israelite high priest similar and different from Jesus Christ entering into the Holy of Holies? (Read Hebrews 9:11-18.)

_____

_____

_____

47) How can we approach God?

_____

48) What was required under the Old Covenant as proof of death? (Read Hebrews 9:16-18.)

_____

49) How do we receive salvation and our eternal inheritance?

_____

> **The Son suffered, as did the Father and the Spirit. No matter how long we study, I am certain we have hardly begun to understand the preciousness of the Blood of Jesus Christ.**

Abraham didn't ask, "Why?" He obeyed. He trusted. He believed. Abraham waged spiritual warfare through obedience.

The scene of Abraham and Isaac on Mt. Moriah stirs strong emotions. There's a sigh of relief when the angel restrains Abraham's hand from plunging the knife into Isaac. Yet, our Father did not spare His only Son whom He loves with a perfect love. Jesus Christ was fully human and divine. He died for us, because death and the shedding of blood were necessary for our restoration and eternal inheritance. Do we *feel* deep gratitude for God's sacrifice?

Sometimes we're complacent about Jesus Christ's death, as if it didn't really cost God. God is tender, gentle, loving, and sensitive. We serve three Gods in One. What happens to One in the Trinity happens to all. The Son suffered, as did the Father and the Spirit. No matter how long we study, I am certain we have hardly begun to understand the preciousness of the Blood of Jesus Christ.

50) How would you reply to the question, "Why do you pray the Blood of Jesus?"

_____

_____

_____

_____

_____

The Blood of Jesus proved He became my substitute. The penalty for my sinfulness was death, but Jesus substituted His life for mine. I can now approach God because of the Blood of Jesus. The Blood of Jesus purchased my freedom. The Blood of Jesus forgave my sins. The Blood of Jesus restored my inheritance.

In the following chapter, we will explore our inheritance.

PART ONE

LESSON THREE

INHERITANCE

Inheritance study is a twofold equipping, helping you live a full life and pray with a demonstration of Holy Spirit power. A lack of understanding regarding our inheritance in Christ results in a power deficit. We have an inheritance in Christ that equips us to overcome personal challenges and pray with results. Conditions governing human inheritance imitate supernatural requirements for receiving our divine birthright. Pray for Holy Spirit understanding of your inheritance through Jesus Christ as you begin.

Ed's mother, Erna, received a certified letter informing her that an unknown relative had died in Germany. A search to find the nearest relative located Erna in the United States. She had to prove she was Erna Eckart. She sent photocopies of personal papers and her notarized signature. German lawyers verified her identity and advised her to expect a check by certified mail. We eagerly watched for the letter to see what amount Erna had received.

Those who have received Jesus Christ as their substitute qualify to receive an inheritance. (Read Colossians 1:12.) God's promise of inheritance generates excitement. God's inheritance is given to those living the exchanged life.

1) Are you curious about the inheritance Jesus Christ left you? Are you eager to receive it? What do you think your inheritance contains?

_____

_____

_____

2) Receiving an inheritance is conditional. Have you ever received an inheritance, or are you aware of being named in a will?

_____

In studying Old Testament covenants, we noticed blood was required as proof of death.

3) What happens before an heir can receive an inheritance? (Read Hebrews 9:16-18.)

_____

_____

We inherited death through Adam. Jesus took our eternal death penalty, as our substitute, at the cross. (Read 1Corinthians 15:21-22.)

4) 1Corinthians 15:21-22 makes reference to the "resurrection of the dead" and says in Christ we will "be made alive." What do you understand these phrases to mean? (See also Romans 5:14-18.)

_____

_____

5) What does John 3:16-17 say? (Read John 3:16-17.)

_____

_____

John 3:16 -17 says God sent His Son Jesus Christ to save the world. The translation of "save" is key to understanding our inheritance. "Save" in John 3:17 is a translation of the Greek word sozo (sode'-zo). Sozo means saved and has other interpretations as well.

Jack Hayford translates "sozo" to mean save, heal, cure, preserve, keep safe and sound, rescue from danger and destruction, deliver, save from physical death by healing and from spiritual death by forgiving sin and its effect. Additional translations of sozo are give new life, cause to have a new heart, protect, do well, make whole, prosper.

> **The translation of "save" is key to understanding our inheritance.**

The Amplified Bible says, "For God so greatly loved *and* dearly prized the world that He [even] gave up His only begotten (unique) Son, so that whoever believes in (trusts in, clings to, relies on) Him shall not perish (come to destruction, be lost) but have eternal (everlasting) life. For God did not send the Son into the world in order to judge (to reject, to condemn, to pass sentence on) the world, but that the world might find salvation *and* be made safe *and* sound through Him."

If you are sharing in a group, share the various translations of John 3:16-17. If you are studying independently, read and compare another translation of John 3:16-17.

6) Using your choice of translation, personalize John 3:16-17. Replace "the world" with your name. Choose other meanings of "sozo" and add them into your personalized scripture verse.

_____

_____

_____

_____

_____

I testify to sozo power at work in my life after a car accident in 2002. We were rear-ended and the car was considered totaled, weeks before our mission to Australia. Seven people came down to the hospital in the middle of the night to pray for Ed and me. I had very severe lower back pain and couldn't turn my head. I felt every muscle had ripped in my neck. After prayer, my lower back pain went and I was able to turn my head!

We had tickets for Australia. As the numbing produced by trauma wore off injuries surfaced, including intense pain. (The specific lower back pain didn't return!) When I prayed about our upcoming trip the Lord gave me a word from Ezekiel 3:22. Paraphrased, the verses say, *the Lord's hand was upon me. God said come out and I will meet you on the plain and I'll speak to you. So I got up and went. The glory of the Lord was there.*

Ed and I had been praying about traveling to a plain in the center of Australia. I felt God affirmed our trip through this scripture, and I expected to meet the Lord in the stillness of the Australian desert plain in a new way.

When our travel day arrived Ed ordered a wheelchair. The airline attendant wheeled me into their private club while we waited to board. I transferred from the wheelchair and stretched out on a lounge facing a central fountain in the room. The normal tensions in the hustle-bustle of an air terminal receded in the peaceful lounge. The Lord reassured me. We boarded to find God provided three seats across on the flight so I could lie down during the ride!

As I walked down the aisle preparing to deplane in Sydney, I heard in my spirit, "Didn't I say I'd meet you on the plane?" I laughed out loud. Surely, He personally met every need. Plain or plane—God's sozo power and His glory surround us!

7) Where have you seen sozo power at work in your life?

_____

_____

_____

Jesus Christ gave believers a four part inheritance:
1) Salvation
2) Healing
3) Deliverance
4) Prosperity

How certain are you of your inheritance? Bette, a dear friend who has gone to the Lord, exemplified a person certain of her inheritance in both heaven and earth.

Bette loved Jesus. Each week she held a full day prayer meeting in her home. One Wednesday at her prayer meeting she pulled out an envelope with a lawyer's return address. A relative had died and Bette had been told to expect an inheritance. She asked everyone at the gathering to pray her inheritance would come quickly. Bette started shopping. She purchased a diamond estate ring in the letter B, bought a white Cadillac, and signed a construction contract for a sunroom addition on her house! Bette started making plans for eight of us from the prayer group to accompany her on a European pilgrimage. She asked us to clear our calendars for certain dates, and she inquired about ticket prices, hotels, etc. She may have been a bit premature in her purchases.

Weeks passed and the longed for letter didn't come. She begged, "*Please, please* pray the check comes quickly!" Even though she didn't have the evidence of her inheritance check in her hand, Bette believed the lawyers. She had it on good authority and trusted the money would come through. People around her knew she had come into money. She made no secret of her inheritance, and her new purchases made it obvious she'd received substantial money.

In the same way, if we believe in Jesus Christ, our lives are characterized by a manifestation of our inheritance. Our inheritance is not for heaven alone, but to impact our generation and future generations. Bette's conversation and lifestyle changes showed she had definitely inherited.

8) How does your conversation and lifestyle demonstrate your belief in your inheritance through Jesus Christ?

_____

_____

John 3:16-17 tells us Jesus came to provide us with a rich inheritance of salvation, healing, deliverance, and prosperity. Erna asked the German lawyers to explain her inheritance. Bette asked the lawyer what amount of money she could expect. We ask our Advocate, the Holy Spirit, to give us a deeper revelation of the meaning of our inheritance.

9) Erna and Bette had full confidence concerning their inheritances. I've met many who hope their inheritance through Christ is true, but aren't sure. Are you confident or doubtful of your inheritance through Christ? What gives you confidence? What causes doubt?

_____

_____

10) Seasons of life present different needs. Your Father has prepared an inheritance for you to meet all of your needs. What do you need today? Can you see how your inheritance in Christ has anticipated your need?

_____

_____

_____

_____

_____

SALVATION

Receiving personal redemption and Holy Spirit revelation of salvation is the first part of our inheritance and empowers us to be vessels of healing. Our inheritance of salvation through Jesus Christ is foundational to the healing ministry. Jesus Christ became our substitute, took our punishment for our sin, and restored us to the Father. We teach salvation through the cross during healing services, personal prayer ministry, and ministry to the dying. I recommend Bridge for Peace CD "Doorkeeper to the House of God" for further exploration of salvation and the healing ministry.

When praying with people for healing, I often ask in a casual tone, "You know where you are going when you die, right?" People sometimes seem a bit surprised by the question. Yet, they sense my sincere interest. For example, I remember Dr. J.

A gracious woman, brown hair and eyes, a specialist, came for prayer. Dr. J told me Jesus had blessed her. She was an immigrant and it was not easy to be licensed in her specialty field in her new country. She had a lengthy testimony to the glory of God. She attributed her current position as a specialist in the hospital to the providence of God.

She had read about the healing service in her church announcements. Dr. J's demanding profession meant long hours, plus she had a husband and children at home, leaving little discretionary time. "I never have time to attend extra church activities, but I knew I was coming today. Then a friend called me last night, suggesting I attend. I knew God was reminding me!"

She had been experiencing a problem walking up and down steps or inclines. "It's very embarrassing at the hospital." She also had some problem with her throat. It was time for prayer. I asked if I could put my hand on her shoulder. With permission, I placed my hand on her shoulder and asked, "You know where you're going when you die, right?" Instantly, tears welled up in her eyes. After her testimony to Jesus Christ, one might expect she knew of her inheritance of salvation. I found, however, she was full of fear. I spoke with her about Jesus Christ. We prayed together, recommitting our lives to God. She also received the Baptism of the Holy Spirit.

Then I asked Dr. J about her throat. She pressed around her throat and found it was healed. She was amazed. We walked to the side of the gymnasium, bleachers lined the wall. She started walking up and down, up and down the bleachers. Dr. J was stunned. She had no limitation at all!

We serve people when we ask about their salvation experience.

11) Are you confident of your salvation in Jesus Christ?

_____

_____

If you are uncertain about where you are going after death, please contact bridgeforpeace@optonline.net. We would like to speak with you.

As ministers of healing, we may have opportunity to minister to the dying. God has used us in many ways at this critical juncture. We have seen some rise up and live to confound the medical community. However, we know everyone will die someday if the Lord has not yet returned. Death can be a time of struggle. Satan often torments people who are dying, tempting them with fear and doubt. Sometimes God's children, who called on the Name of Jesus throughout their lives, forget the covenant when death draws near. We minister the truth of Jesus Christ's cross and remind them of their inheritance.

My friend Yetta, who was under five feet and over eighty years of age, frequently urged me, "Hold the rope, darling. Hold the rope!" Her warning reminded me of the expression "Jesus is our anchor behind the veil." In Christian art an anchor symbolizes hope. After death my eyes will be opened and I will see behind "the veil". Now, I am too spiritually "short-sighted". At times of spiritual illumination, I catch glimpses when the veil seems like a gossamer wisp. At other times, I cannot even see the veil! What is beyond death is imperfectly seen, but I know Jesus has gone before me beyond the veil. He is my anchor, my hope, having passed through death into new life. Through Christ's resurrection, we have a real hope.

I find the anchor image helpful when praying with those who are about to die. I also find God often gives me precious glimpses of heaven to share when ministering to the dying. I simply relate what I see. Describing how I see Jesus as our anchor behind the veil brings great comfort. I see Jesus already there and as I hold onto the three-fold cord of the Father, Son, and Holy Spirit I will arrive in heaven, the unseen place, where I will see Jesus face to face.

12) How would you explain Jesus as your anchor behind the veil?
(Read Hebrews 6:19-20.)

_____

_____

_____

Ed and I ministered to a man in his eighties on his hospital deathbed. He loved the Lord. His wife said he had always been afraid to die and was lingering. He was unconscious. His hands were swollen from intravenous; he was connected to many tubes and suffering. He was restless. Ed and I arrived to pray for him. The family left the room. We reminded him of the covenant of love he had entered into with Jesus Christ. The curtain had been torn for him. We reminded him that Jesus had gone before him as his anchor behind the veil.

We left the hospital room and spoke with the adult children in the hall. The wife went to her dying husband. She came back into the hallway and asked, "What did you say to him? He's at peace now." He went to the Lord that night.

I ministered to a woman who was lingering for weeks on her deathbed. The family said she had no peace. I reminded her of the agreement God had made with her when she gave her life to Jesus. I reminded her of her inheritance. She died peacefully that evening.

Another woman we ministered to was in great pain on her deathbed. After reminding her of the Blood of Jesus, the loving God she'd served, the God she would be reunited with in heaven, her body relaxed and she went that day to meet her Savior.

Perhaps these witnesses reminded you of a testimony from your own life.

13) Record your testimony here.

_____

_____

_____

_____

These testimonies demonstrate the importance of speaking to people about the New Covenant, the Blood of Jesus, and their inheritance when praying for the sick and ministering to the dying.

HEALING

Scriptural knowledge of our inheritance empowers us to release Holy Spirit power for healing. Increasing in understanding of God's Word and in knowledge of our healing inheritance helps us grow more effective in prayer ministry.

Many of the following testimonies are letters from View from the Bridge, the Bridge for Peace publication. If you would like to receive View from the Bridge contact us at bridgeforpeace@optonline.net.

Terry complained of pain at level seven on a scale of one to ten—ten being the worst. She had arthritic pain in her back. The team prayed with her and her pain lowered to a three. Then after more prayer she declared her back and knee pain were completely gone.

Alex said he was at a party and was roughhousing with his teenage friends. They were older and bigger than him and he got the worst of it. After, he had terrible shooting pains in his wrist every time he moved it. A few weeks went by and it still hurt. He was concerned because he plays on a baseball team. His mother prayed for him and he was a little better, but it still hurt a lot. Finally, his parents told him he wouldn't be allowed to play baseball or go to baseball camp if the pain didn't stop. He came to a Bridge for Peace service and his wrist was healed. He had a baseball game the next day and his wrist was fine and has been great ever since. He gives praise to Jesus Christ.

Claire had nodules on her thyroid. As Ed prayed for her she felt the nodules shrink. Claire brought along Kate, her two-and-a-half-year-old daughter. Kate sat on her mother's lap and listened as Ed invoked the power of the Blood of Jesus. Later, Claire mentioned that Kate had been awake most of the night because of tooth pain. Ed asked Kate for permission to touch her face. She shyly nodded. Ed prayed for Kate to be free from tooth pain in the name of Jesus through the Blood Covenant. When they went home, Kate said her tooth pain was all gone. She asked her mother, "Who was that doctor that touched my face and made the pain go away?" Claire explained that Ed was not a doctor, but a man who loved Jesus very much.

We have seen cancer healed, tumors vanish, the crippled walk, the blind see, the deaf hear, and the mute speak as a result of the Blood of Jesus and the inheritance He gives us.

14) God acts marvelously through those who serve Him. Write your personal testimony of a healing you witnessed or received.

_____

_____

_____

_____

_____

_____

_____

_____

DELIVERANCE

It is our responsibility to pray for deliverance as well as healing. Ed and I attended a conference on spiritual warfare in the 1990s. The well-known minister of healing, Francis MacNutt, was the main speaker. He begged, "Please, get into the deliverance ministry. People are dying out there."

Freedom from fears and addictions comes through the power of the Blood. Minister the Blood Covenant of Jesus Christ, eternal life through Him, and the certainty of being created for God's express and glorious purpose to the despairing, depressed, and those plagued by suicidal thoughts. At the time of this writing, in the United States the second leading cause of death in teenagers is suicide. Those who suffer mental illness need medical and psychological help. As Christians, we must do our job of praying for deliverance for those in mental torment.

Many people are involved in occult activities. These include horoscopes, palm reading, astrology, fortune tellers, numerology, ouija boards and satanic worship. Some are victims of ritualistic satanic abuse. On Long Island, New York, there are areas where mutilated animals used in satanic cult worship are found on a regular basis. There are churches listed in the yellow pages in the United States for satanic worship. The Holy Spirit works through us to release deliverance through the Blood of Jesus Christ.

Bridge for Peace visited a church in Australia. Maya, a severely depressed lady, began to receive her healing as I spoke about what Jesus did for us at the cross. The moment I stepped down from the sanctuary, she ran up the aisle to me and said, "I'd forgotten about the Blood of Jesus." She had been suffering with severe depression for several years. Maya underwent a transformation as she heard again what Jesus had done for her at the cross. Several years later, I met her again. She had been healed of depression since the reminder of the Blood of Jesus.

I prayed for a woman who had been involved in voodoo. Her eyes appeared glazed. She was gripped with a fear that she would never be released from the power of satan worshipers. She had been told by Christian ministers that she was "not going to make it". I disagreed, saying, "Everything Jesus Christ said in the Bible says you will 'make it.'" I prayed for her. I watched her eyes clear after some time. She testified Jesus Christ delivered her from demonic power.

Bridge for Peace Uganda prayed for the release of a young boy who had been abducted and forced to serve in the rebel army. Very few of these children are restored to their families. One night, during a Bridge for Peace conference, it was announced that the boy escaped and returned home. His mother screamed and fainted. Other women who had joined her in prayer let out a victory shout.

In Brazil a woman heard of Bridge for Peace ministry and waited for us in the airport as we were departing the country. She was in tremendous pain. She said people involved in witchcraft had cut off the head of a pig and used the blood to put a curse on her. As we prayed for her in the airport, her head twisted, her neck bones made a grinding sound. The spirit said, "I'm going to break her neck." We rebuked the spirit. She was delivered by the Blood of Jesus Christ through team prayer.

15) Did these witnesses remind you of a deliverance testimony from your own life? Record your testimony here.

_____

_____

_____

_____

PROVISION

When we know our inheritance we pray with confidence for provision. God backs His Word with power.

Bridge for Peace teams prayed for a woman who had lost her job and subsequently experienced depression. She felt the joy of the Lord after prayer. She came back the next week to testify that her company phoned her and offered her a job with a pay increase.

Bridge for Peace teams prayed for T, a man who was second in command of a company that employed hundreds and provided care for children. Fraudulent practices were uncovered. The CEO's whereabouts could not be discovered. T knew he would be held responsible by the federal investigators. Bridge for Peace prayed for T. He was exonerated and the company was put on six month probation before their contract would be resumed. T and his wife called the Bridge for Peace office to testify to the power of God. They said it was miraculous!

Bridge for Peace teams have visited dozens of countries. Ed and I have numerous stories of how God has miraculously provided for these trips. From the smallest detail to the largest need, God provides for us through our inheritance in Jesus Christ.

> **Isaiah 53:4-5 tells us Jesus is our Bridge for Peace.**

16) Record a provision testimony here.

_____

_____

_____

SCRIPTURAL INHERITANCE

Jesus often quoted scripture when He taught (Matthew 12:40), when He corrected people (Matthew 15:8), or when He battled satan (Matthew 4:4). When you pray for people, include scripture as the Holy Spirit brings verses to mind. The Bible is filled with promises of our inheritance, salvation, healing, deliverance, and provision.

Isaiah 53:4-5 often comes to my mind when I'm praying for someone. Isaiah prophesies the coming of Jesus, the correction for our peace. We live the fulfillment of the prophecy. To me, the verses say Jesus is our Bridge for Peace. Wonderful healings begin when people hear the truth expressed in Isaiah 53 and begin to realize whatever their circumstances, Jesus is the answer, the cure, the correction for their peace.

Is there a scripture about inheritance, salvation, healing, deliverance or provision that comes to your mind? Perhaps you have a long history with a particular scripture. Maybe the Holy Spirit is drawing you to something new. God may be inviting you to make the verses your own. Meditate upon it and let it fill your spirit. God may lead you to use the verse in prayer. The living Word of God penetrates to the heart and provides healing. Let the Word live in you. It's not a matter of quoting scripture word for word. The question is whether or not the Word is alive in you.

17) Select a scripture verse regarding either inheritance or one of the four aspects of inheritance we have discussed. How might you pray this scripture with a person in need?

_____

_____

_____

<u>NOTES</u>

_____

_____

_____

_____

_____

_____

_____

_____

_____

_____

_____

_____

_____

_____

_____

_____

_____

PART ONE

LESSON FOUR

WHY DID JESUS DIE FOR US?

This lesson explores the question "Why did Jesus die for us?" We probe the "Why?" with particular attention to the healing ministry. Jesus died to free us from past sin through forgiveness and to secure our eternal life with God forever in heaven after death. We exchange an eternity in hell for eternity in heaven through Jesus Christ. God established a covenant through the cross, but action is required on our behalf. If we covenant with Christ, to be faithful to the covenant, our lives must demonstrate *"exchanged life"* power. He equips Christians through the exchanged life—He gave His life for us, we give our life to Him. Christ's death empowers us to participate in ushering in His Second Coming. The New Covenant requires our participation in preparing for Christ's return. After you complete this course, I encourage you to continue to pursue the question "Why?" The answers lead to glory after glory.

John 3:16 gives an answer to "Why?" Love. God *so loved* the world. The Father, Son, and Holy Spirit love you. The outflow of love is to desire intimacy. Jesus Christ's cross bridged the gap between God and man restoring the possibility of intimate relationship, satisfying the yearnings of God and man.

Jesus Christ died to secure our salvation through the forgiveness of sins (Hebrews 9:12). The Blood of Jesus cleanses us from every sin (1John 1:7). God offers salvation to all who embrace Jesus Christ as Lord and repent of past sins. God changes our hearts. We are reborn through the Blood of Jesus as children of God, heirs of a new inheritance. We desire to adhere to God's Word. Our thoughts and behavior reflect the transformation.

Jesus gave His life so we could have new life. The following scriptures describe our new life through Jesus.
   John 8:36 says new life will be a liberated life, set free from sin.
   John 10:10 says new life will be full, abundant life.
   John 15:11 says new life will be life of true joy.
   John 16:33 says new life will give inner peace despite times of outer turmoil.

1) Is your life characterized by freedom, abundance, joy, and peace as promised in John's gospel? Explain your answer.

_____

_____

God promises freedom, abundance, joy, and peace in our new life. When I say "Jesus is Lord" (Acts 2:36) I speak from a personal perspective. I reject satan's lordship, I exert my right to choose Jesus Christ. Choosing Jesus Christ means asking Him to be Lord of my life.

Some never receive God's promises for two reasons. First, a false belief that, though I say Jesus is Lord, I can still make my own life choices. Second, proclaiming Jesus Christ as Lord, but failing to move from Old Covenant to New.

> **Salvation is the exchanged life, Christ alive in us.**

Proclaiming Jesus as Lord means I have given God my life. It is a dangerous delusion to clutch independence to our hearts, glorify self-determination and imagine we are entitled to God's blessings. Receiving Christ means acknowledging total dependence on the Trinity. We no longer strive to control our destiny, but know God leads us to fulfill our life's purpose. We die to our old life and are born into a new one. When we receive Jesus as Lord we can say with Paul we have been crucified with Christ and no longer live, but Christ lives in us (Galatians 2:20).

2) What does the phrase to be "crucified with Christ" mean to you?

_____

_____

Many know the Name of Jesus, but still live under the Old Covenant. In the Old Covenant people tried to live up to the law, to keep the rules. Generation after generation failed. The law proved we had no power to keep it. The apostle Paul teaches us how the Law showed him his need for Jesus Christ (Romans 7).

Paul confronted his contemporaries. He urged them to consider the implications of the New Covenant and ride the wave of grace released through the power of the cross. Paul was resisted, but he persisted. (Read Colossians 2:13-14.)

3) Have you experienced pressure to appear "Christian" and conform to an external standard?

_____

4) Have you found external "Christian" standards to be life giving—offering you more joy, peace, inner freedom, a sense of abundance?

_____

Grace from the cross of Jesus Christ is the only way to victory over sin.

5) Have you ever struggled to overcome repetitive sin by trying harder? What was your experience?

_____

6) How would you differentiate between God's law written on your heart and striving to live up to an external standard?

_____

_____

_____

We need the New Covenant. The New Covenant is more than the lip service of calling Jesus Lord. Salvation is the exchanged life, Christ alive in us. The voice of God comes alive within, guiding, warning, loving, and contradicting the voice of judgment, self-condemnation, and accusation. The voice of God dismantles lies that have distorted our self-image and gently, persistently urges us toward abundant life.

We hear conflicting voices in our minds. The Holy Spirit whispers truth. Satan pressures and bullies us to influence our choices. Memories of exhilarating successes and painful failures train us to follow established patterns of behavior.

> **The voice of God dismantles lies that have distorted our self-image and gently, persistently urges us toward abundant life.**

7) When have you risked change in response to God's voice in your life? What was the outcome?

_____

_____

_____

_____

Jesus came to cleanse us from our sin by washing us in His Blood. Our just God required atonement for our sin, a prerequisite for reconciliation. Why did Jesus die for us? We rightfully say, "Jesus died for our sins." We correctly say, "Jesus died to secure our place in heaven with Him." We must press further into the question. If our understanding stops here we will *never* live the victorious life God intended for us.

Salvation, forgiveness of sin, new birth makes us children of God. Grasp this truth. Jesus came to cleanse us from our sins by washing us with His Blood. He did not come to present our sin to His Father. Jesus died on the cross to present us, to present *our lives,* as a special gift to His Father. He purchased for us eternal life in heaven and owns our present lives on earth.

We could only be restored to God through blood sacrifice. Jesus became our blood sacrifice. Recognizing Jesus Christ's power to save, we ask Him to become our Savior and Lord. Entering into the Blood Covenant, we live the exchanged life. Acknowledging that He gave His life for us, we give our lives to Him. If we refuse to give Him our lives, then we forfeit the supernatural gifts of freedom, abundance, joy, and peace.

> **Jesus died on the cross to present *us*, to present *our lives,* as a special gift to His Father.**

Through Jesus Christ's death we are restored to the Father. Restoration means we are reinstated as adopted sons and daughters of God, though we still live in the fallen world. God begins to reveal Himself to us, leading us to deeper love for Him and truer worship of Him. In Christ-like obedience, our hearts whisper the Son's words, "Here I am, I have come to do your will." (Hebrews 10:9).

8) In what ways have you noticed your submission to the will of God growing in your life?

_____

_____

_____

9) Where do you find your will in conflict with God's choice for you?

_____

_____

1John 3:16 and 22 say we will progressively recognize, perceive, and understand God's essential love displayed at the cross. As this occurs, we grow to serve sacrificially as He served us. God's call on Bridge for Peace is healing to the nations. We worship and serve God and others through the laying on of hands for the healing of the sick, encouragement of the discouraged, and empowerment of the oppressed. Jesus has the healing ministry, we have a servant ministry.

Why did Jesus die for us? We've touched on the exchanged life crucial for salvation, receiving God's promises, and fulfilling our destiny. Christ's healing flows from His cross.

Various types of healing characterize Jesus Christ's ministry. People received inner healing of emotional wounds (John 4:17-29). Physical healings of eyes, ears, bones, etc. typified His ministry. Jesus also healed by establishing right livelihood—fishermen became preachers, lepers and demoniacs were restored to society. Cheats and authority abusers repented and turned to right livelihood. Jesus healed by restoring dignity to and through work as demonstrated in the life of Zacchaeus and the disciples (Luke 19:1-9, Luke 10:7). Zacchaeus' profession was scorned, because tax collectors were known to be unscrupulous. When Jesus called Zacchaeus, he repented and determined to conduct his work with honor. As a trustworthy employee, he glorified God: esteeming himself and his office as tax collector. There is a tremendous need for healing in the workplace.

Jesus Christ continues His healing ministry through us when we live the exchanged life. His death made it possible to send Christians (His Body) into the world to heal and deliver. Jesus said those who believe in Him would do greater works "because I go to the Father." (John 14:12) Jesus died for us that we might do the greater works, glorifying Him and His Father.

10) In what one way does God continue His healing ministry through you?

_____

_____

_____

You reach others through and for Christ when you serve in healing ministry. Jesus told us to expect greater works through the Body of Christ because of His death.

Jesus also died for us to send us the Holy Spirit. Jesus says in John 16:7 that His death was to our advantage, because He would send the Holy Spirit to us.

11) If you have given your life to Christ then you can agree with Paul's words in Galatians 2:20. Write the scripture here inserting your own name.

_____

_____

_____

Jesus died for us, substituted His death for our death penalty, to give us eternal life. Some people believe we are to suffer on earth until we receive our reward in heaven. This course shows Jesus died in order that we would *live* for Him and impact our generation for Him.

Foundation for Healing

Part Two

PART TWO

LESSON ONE

AUTHORITY I

We have authority because we are under authority. We study our God-given authority knowing our right to act in the Name of Jesus will be tested. Jesus Christ's authority was challenged. "By whose authority do you..." (Matthew 21:23). He restored people's sight, hearing, and mobility. Christ was transparent about His beliefs, genuine in His love, brilliant in His teaching, and still people grumbled asking, essentially, "Who gave Him the right? Who does He think He is?" Jesus demonstrated in word and action that He clearly understood authority. We must grow to understand our Christ-given authority to succeed in our life-given purpose and to give Christ glory as we serve in healing ministry.

AUTHORITY of the NAME of JESUS

We scheduled a Bridge for Peace prayer walk at the United Nations. A woman employed by the United Nations heard of our plans and asked Ed to contact her. She told him, "Use my name."

When the Bridge for Peace team arrived at the UN, Ed called her on the internal lobby phone. She authorized a security guard to take us into restricted areas we would not have accessed if we hadn't been able to "use" her name. In a similar way, the Name of Jesus opens doors for us. Jesus Christ gives us entry into heaven. Without His Name there is no salvation.

Jesus has given us His Name in a legal covenant agreement. He has given us His Name, the authority to act on His behalf, as in a *power of attorney*.

When Ed and I went on mission to the Philippines, the State Department issued a high alert for two areas on our itinerary. We empowered my brother Kevin to act on our behalf in the event that our return to the US was delayed. Through a legal document called a *power of attorney* we fully authorized Kevin to represent us in any legal concerns that might occur in our absence. We trusted Kevin completely because of our relationship.

Relationship is the key to trust. We believed Kevin knew our mindset and would exert authority to implement our wishes to the best of his ability in any circumstance because of our relationship.

As Christ's authorized representatives we come to know God's will through prayer, Bible study, and other ways God speaks with us. As God's will is revealed, we act accordingly. The Spirit helps us grow in knowledge and understanding of God's Word and covenant. Through grace we enforce the authority of the Name of Jesus.

Those studying in group, compare translations of Philippians 2:8 at your meeting. If you are doing an independent study, look up another translation of Philippians 2:8.

1) Paraphrase Philippians 2:8-11.

_____

_____

_____

2) Scripture says Jesus' Name is above every name. What does that mean to you?

_____

_____

God's followers are authorized to use the Name of Jesus. With the privilege comes responsibility. To help us understand our position in the Kingdom of God, Paul uses a metaphor likening our work to a government ambassador's esteemed position. When we use the Name of Jesus Christ we exert God's power and authority as Christ's ambassadors. (Read 2Corinthians 5:20.)

3) Accepting Paul's description of a Christian as an ambassador for Christ, how would you define your responsibility?

_____

_____

_____

4) Note an occasion when you acted as an ambassador for Christ or a present situation where you sense an opportunity to act as God's ambassador.

_____

_____

_____

> **We need "God-assurance", not self-assurance.**

People in authoritarian government and church positions tried to intimidate Jesus on many occasions. Jesus never avoided confrontation. Confident in His authority, Jesus models "God-assurance" when dealing with conflict from every level of society. We need "God-assurance", not self-assurance. God-assurance causes us to boldly stand our ground when challenged. God assures us He gives us His authority through scripture.

5) What does Jesus say about authority? (Read Matthew 28:18-20.)

_____

_____

_____

6) What kind of authority and diplomatic immunity did Jesus give his followers? (Read Luke 10:19, Mark 16:17-18.)

_____

_____

_____

The Pharisees, a religious sect, threatened Jesus and tried to intimidate Him with Herod's authority. Herod was the provincial governor. He had murdered John the Baptist and had the power to execute Jesus. Jesus warned His disciples to guard themselves from the power of intimidation and insinuation. He cautioned them to reject religious and governmental hypocrisy (Luke 12:1).

In Luke 13:31, we find the Pharisees practicing the hypocrisy Jesus warned about. While appearing to caution Him about Herod, they were actually threatening Him. They despised Jesus and wished Him dead.

Jesus responds with authority, proving His God-assurance.

7) What does Jesus say about Himself when threatened with death?
(Read Luke 13:31-33.)

_____

_____

_____

Jesus shows us how to stand our ground. He knows what He has come to do and knows He has authority to accomplish it.

Jesus personally gave the apostles their authority. Paul never had the privilege to meet Jesus when He walked on the earth. We have that in common with him. Yet, Paul knew his competence in Christ. Paul breathed God-assurance. How encouraging for us. We can be like Paul, certain of our God-given authority.

8) How can we be assured of our effectiveness for Christ? (Read 2Corinthians 3:4-6.)

_____

_____

_____

9) How would you assess your God-assurance today?

_____

_____

10) How can you nurture God-assurance growth? Consider your daily responsibilities before answering. If you keep in mind your obligations, this answer can be valuable in helping you develop a personal plan to foster spiritual growth.

_____

_____

_____

Jesus says He will be healing people and driving demons out today and tomorrow (Luke 13:32-33). Jesus Christ continues His work through us. Pray in His Name, authorized, commissioned, and empowered to lay hands on people for healing and deliverance. Enforce God's finished work at the cross today. Jesus Christ's response to the Pharisees foreshadows His coming resurrection. Until Jesus Christ returns, we take authority over sickness and demons in His Name.

11) What did Jesus' followers say about demons? (Read Luke 10:17.)

_____

_____

AUTHORITY TO SET CAPTIVES FREE

Demonization occurred in biblical times and still happens today. According to Jesus Christ, casting out demons is part of our Christian commission. We may have a 9-5 job in an office, but we also have the work of casting out demons as ambassadors of Christ enforcing the authority of the Name of Jesus. Jesus qualifies those He authorizes.

In Australia, I prayed with a young woman I'll call Margaret who was accompanied by her sister Anna. Anna said Margaret had been afflicted for many years by demons. She would be thrown to the ground suddenly, while riding a bus or walking along the street. Her sister said, "If Margaret tries to read the Bible the demons throw her around."
I asked Margaret, "Do you want to be set free?"

"Yes."

Anna said, "She's been prayed for before. Do you want to know the names of the demons?"

"No," I answered. "The only name I need to know is Jesus Christ. Margaret, pray after me. 'Father, I come to you in the Name of Jesus'." Healing ministry is reliance on the Holy Spirit, not a formula. When driving out a spirit, Jesus asked it to give its name. (Read Mark 5:9.) *Many* times, Jesus did not ask the spirit's name. It is not necessary to ask the demonic spirit's name, it is necessary to rely on the Holy Spirit as to how to proceed. In Margaret's case, as in most cases, I did not feel led to ask the spirit's name.

When Margaret prayed, "the Name of Jesus", tormenting spirits threw her down and she thrashed on the floor. I crouched down on the ground and prayed, repeating "In the Name of Jesus" until she was able to pray, "In the Name of Jesus." Finally, she sat up. We continued to pray and came to the phrase "I am cleansed by the Blood of Jesus Christ." Again, Margaret was thrown to the floor. She rolled and thrashed as I repeated, "I am cleansed by the Blood of Jesus Christ."

Having studied the Blood Covenant in Part One, we have some understanding of cleansing through the Blood. Satan does not want us to speak in the Name of Jesus or talk about the cleansing Blood. Demons recognize authority in the Name of Jesus Christ. They recognize believers' "power of attorney" and do not want us to exercise the power of the Name of Jesus Christ.

People had gathered at the disturbance to watch the manifestation. I discourage people from focusing on demonic manifestation. Demons want to draw our attention away from God. I encourage people to stay in their seats and continue to pray for whatever God is doing in the service. However, my work is to pray for the captive to be set free. If people who've been instructed to pray run forward to watch what's happening, I ignore them and persist in prayer for the one in need.

The Blood of Jesus set Margaret free after a period of demonic resistance. The group witnessed her deliverance to God's glory!

Margaret and I sat on the floor. Recalling what Anna had said about the demons preventing Margaret from reading the Bible, I handed her the scriptures and asked her to read. People sat down, encircling her. She read from John's gospel, her voice soft and childlike, "...you will be unshakable and assured, deeply at peace."

The media has sensationalized the demonic, producing horror movies and television shows. Jesus and His disciples dealt with demons as a matter of fact, not fiction. If you are a disciple of Jesus, God has given you authority over demons.

12) How do you feel about the deliverance ministry?

_____

_____

_____

_____

AUTHORITY TO HEAL

While visiting a church office Ed met Alice, the head secretary. She had a torn rotator cuff, was in constant pain, and couldn't raise her arm. Surgery was scheduled and she'd been advised to expect a six-month recovery. She had an appointment with the physical therapist that afternoon.

Ed asked, "Would you like me to pray for you?"

"Yes!"

Ed used his "power of attorney" as Christ's commissioned ambassador. Ed carried out God's command. He spoke to the circumstance of Alice's shoulder in the Name of Jesus. "Try it out," Ed advised.

Her arm rose easily, without any discomfort. Alice was stunned. She went to her physical therapist that afternoon and lifted her arm into the air. Her therapist said, "You can't do that!"

In the Name of Jesus Christ Alice's rotator cuff surgery was cancelled. God commands His ambassadors to exercise supernatural authority for His glory.

13) Record an instance when you saw the authority of the Name of Jesus enforced and a healing resulted.

_____

_____

_____

PART TWO

LESSON TWO

AUTHORITY II

Our study continues to focus on authority through the powerful Name of Jesus. We begin to explore issues surrounding power. We examine our experiences, because our feelings about power can influence our fruitfulness in prayer. If you believe in Jesus, God has chosen *you*, appointed *you* to fulfill His purpose, commanded *you* to bear lasting fruit. Jesus connects fruitfulness with answered prayer. God gives us authority. We use authority in obedience to the Holy Spirit to produce results that glorify God (John 15:16).

IMPORTANCE OF A NAME

Several scripture passages show us names are important. God tells Abram He will confirm His covenant with him. Abram falls face down before the Lord. This is the first instance of Abram prostrating Himself to worship the Lord. God then changes Abram's name to Abraham (Father of Nations) (Genesis 17:5). Abram's wife Sarai became Sarah (Genesis 17:15). The couple had attempted to fulfill God's Word through human means, but grew to trust God's ability to fulfill His purpose for them in miraculous ways. They received new names after their characters had been tested and approved. Abraham proves his strong faith through the episode concerning Isaac's sacrifice, as already discussed.

> **God's Name and God's Presence are synonymous.**

Jacob was renamed after a rite-of-passage testing (Genesis 32:24-28). God renamed Jacob (deceiver) and he became Israel (one who struggles with God and man and prevails).

Isaiah said the Lord called him from the womb; and "from the body of my mother He has named my name." (Isaiah 49:1b) We, too, have been created by God, called from the womb and named by God.

Customarily, Jewish children received a first name from their ancestors. In the naming of John the Baptist, God intervened, giving direction that broke with convention. Zechariah was told by an angel to name his son John, though people remarked on the break with tradition (Luke 1:13, 60-63). John means "God is favorable". Certainly, God's favor was toward His people when He sent John as the forerunner to Jesus.

The Word says an angel of the Lord appeared to Joseph in a dream to reassure him and tell him the name He was to give Mary's child. "And you shall call His Name Jesus." (Matthew 1:21) Jesus is Greek for the Hebrew name Joshua, which means Savior.

Bridge for Peace Foundation for Healing

1) Why do you think people were renamed or given specific names in the Bible?

_____

_____

_____

2) Write your name and its meaning below. You can often discover the meaning of your name in the dictionary or encyclopedia. Does your name have family significance?

_____

_____

_____

3) In light of our exploration of the importance of a name, what do you think the significance of your name might be?

_____

_____

_____

A name evokes the essence of a person. When we hear the name of someone we know spoken, we react as though the person were there. If we like them, we may smile at the mention of their name. If we love them, we feel emotion. If we dislike them, negative feelings rise up. It's as though the person is there at the mention of their name. When God's name is prayed, He is there with power. Scripture says He is with us when we pray in His name in agreement with others. (Read Matthew 18:19-20.)

4) Have you had an experience when you noticed God's Presence while praying in agreement with others? Record your experience.

_____

_____

_____

God spoke His own Name to Moses (Exodus 3:14). In revealing His Name, God revealed His character, His attributes. God's Name denotes His real Presence.

PRAYING IN THE NAME OF JESUS

Jesus teaches us to pray in His Name and to pray in agreement. (Read Matt 18:19.) Jesus' instruction is not a formula, it is His living Word. God's Word reveals His desires. When we pray in God's Name, we pray according to God's will as revealed to us in scripture. When we pray in Jesus' Name, we pray with God, Who intercedes for us (Romans 8:26-27, 34). God's Name and God's Presence are synonymous. The Holy Spirit inspires, stirs desires, and we pray accordingly.

> **Jesus' instruction is not a formula, it is His living Word.**

5) Read John 14:13-14 and John 16:23-24. Note one or more common themes in these scriptures and discuss what you notice about them.

_____

_____

_____

At times people close their prayer with "…but, Thy will be done." Jesus told us to pray this phrase with faith (Matthew 6:9-10). However, sometimes people negate their prayer by using "Thy will be done" to suggest their prayer may not be the will of God. "Thy will be done" is not an escape clause tacked on the end of prayer as an excuse for fruitless prayer. Jesus prayed "Thy will be done" declaring He preferred God's will above His own desire (Luke 22:42).

Jesus faced torture and ultimate death. He expressed a hope to avoid the horror if possible. However, He knew the Father's will and reconfirmed His determination to conform to it. This is how He prayed "Thy will be done."

When we use this phrase in prayer, we have already sought to know His will, as Jesus did. We pray "Thy will be done" with knowledge of God's will, imitating Jesus. We pray determined to persevere to see the manifestation of God's will, as Jesus determined to persevere through His horrific ordeal to see God's will done.

6) Share an experience of praying "Your will be done."

_____

_____

_____

POWER

Governments exercise authority by establishing territorial boundaries, but without power to protect their borders they are vulnerable to enemy invasion. We are physical and spiritual beings. Territorial boundaries exist in the spiritual realm. Satan battles to keep and gain spiritual territory. Warfare is reality for every disciple of Christ. God gave us spiritual authority to protect our spiritual and physical boundaries. We are not fighting against human beings, but against demonic forces (Ephesians 6:12). God invests His ambassadors with power to back their God-given authority.

ABUSE OF POWER

People respond differently to the concept of power. The word power often triggers strong emotions. Some fear the responsibility of power, others crave power. Victims of abusive power may fear exercising authority. Some Christians feel unworthy to release God's power. They reject God's call to step forward, reach out, and speak authoritatively in the Name of Jesus Christ. Personality tendencies lead some to back up, sit down, and give way. Some people can never satisfy their hunger for power. In our society, many women have been taught power is unladylike. Some churches disempower their members. The result is Christians need healing to step into godly power and authority.

We need the Holy Spirit to teach us and give us wisdom regarding authority and power. Clearly, God expects us to release His supernatural power of love, mercy, healing, and deliverance. God's power brings joy, peace, and harmony. If we refuse our commission, unchecked demonic power will create hell on earth.

7) How do you feel about power?

_____

_____

_____

8) How do you feel about being entrusted with God's power?

_____

_____

_____

Scripture teaches about power. (Read Acts 19:11-17.) In Acts of the Apostles, Jesus has resurrected and ascended to His Father. Paul, a former Christian persecutor, has had a dramatic conversion experience. He understands Old Testament prophets pointed to Jesus Christ as Messiah. He has realized Jesus died to present him to the Father. When Paul prayed, mighty Holy Spirit power coursed through him and miracles flowed. Word spread. People took pieces of Paul's clothing to the sick. After contact with the cloth they were healed! People flocked to Paul. He was sought out by desperate people for healing through Jesus Christ. Opportunists, such as the sons of Sceva, observed Paul, hoping to learn the source of his power.

The Sceva exorcists copied Paul, pronouncing the Name of Jesus over a demonized person. They had a formula, but they had no authority. The evil spirits knew the sons lacked authority. They battered the "professionals." The sons of Sceva, naked and bloody, dashed out of the house.

Irreverent use of the Name of Jesus offends the Lord (Exodus 20:7). God will bring judgment on those who are careless with His Name. Recklessly speaking the Name of Jesus is dangerous profane foolishness. Insincere, self-serving people employing the holy Name of Jesus will suffer grim consequences. A person who is not submitted to God's authority and uses Jesus' Name is guilty of trying to abuse heavenly power.

Opportunists still exploit the Name of Jesus for their own gain. In this sense, opportunist has a negative connotation. It defines a person looking for opportunities to further their own cause, often at others' expense. In this sense, an "opportunist" would be the opposite of a servant of Jesus Christ. They strive to turn healing in the Name of Jesus Christ to personal advantage. They use spiritual gifts to control others, to feed their ego, or for financial gain. Opportunists have scarred many people and caused others to reject Christianity.

I've heard numerous stories about spiritual exploitation. God has established Bridge for Peace in Uganda. Witchdoctors are licensed practitioners there. Some sick people look for healing in the church. If they don't have results they may go to the witchdoctor.

A witchdoctor was converted to Jesus Christ at one of our open air meetings. He testified, revealing tricks of his former trade. He said witchdoctors leave poisoned food alongside trails where people travel. In Uganda, many are hungry. Witchdoctors know people will eat the food and become patients. He told us witchdoctors put bits of poisoned substances under a patient's skin to keep the patient dependent upon them, resulting in a continual flow of cash.

Religious frauds have duped many people into giving them adulation and money.

9) Have you or someone you know experienced spiritual power abuse? Explain.

_____

_____

Professional opportunists exist. Some call themselves Christians, but they are abusers of power. Scammers imitate the sons of Sceva. If you've experienced abusive power by Christians, you may need to forgive and be healed.

10) Has the Holy Spirit reminded you of an area that needs to be healed? Can you forgive the abuser and ask Jesus to heal you?

_____

_____

_____

Many people are fascinated with power and will do anything to get it. They stockpile whatever they think will bring them power. Some gather talismans or worship satan. Some worship money or political power. Some abuse sex for power. Drugs and alcohol make others feel powerful. Some abuse positions in the family, at work, or in the church. Some people use lust for power. They dress, talk, and act in ways to cause people to lust after them, to bring people under their power, or under their "spell."

11) Do you need to ask forgiveness for abusing power? Explain.

_____

_____

_____

_____

You can receive healing today from Jesus Christ. God wants to do extraordinary things for you and through you. We need to receive His power and authority to live out the life God intended for us.

The Name of Jesus, His Blood at the Cross, and God's authority are to be reverenced. God's servants speak His Name in submitted love. Servants of the Most High God owe everything to Him. We minister in humility, properly using authority, giving God all glory. We lay hands on the sick and speak to demons, exercise God's authority and see results.

As God heals our power issues, we grow in expectant faith. Some people come for prayer without expecting much to happen. Sometimes I ask, "Do you want to be healed?" and people respond, "Well, I think so." or, "I hope I could be set free." They haven't begun to understand their position in Christ. Their identity has been robbed.

IDENTITY THEFT

Thieves steal people's identities and run up fraudulent credit card bills. Identity theft is fast growing, but a more heinous crime has been perpetrated. Satan has stolen people's identity in Christ.

We have an identity in Christ restored through the Blood Covenant. Victims of spiritual identity theft do not know who they are in Christ. They haven't begun to understand forgiveness through Jesus' Blood, the blessings of Blood Covenant, or anything about their inheritance. Their giftedness has been obscured, and they're unable to carry out their commission. Those who have had their spiritual identity robbed find Christ's commission burdensome or are self-condemned by it, seeing themselves as failures. They find no satisfaction or joy in God's plan. They lack power to live out their purpose. Identity theft results in ineffectiveness.

> **Victims of spiritual identity theft do not know who they are in Christ.**

12) Has satan tried to rob your identity? What helps? Share your experience.

_____

_____

RIGHTEOUSNESS

Read James 5:16. James says the prayers of a righteous man are powerful and effective. Who is righteous? No one can make themselves righteous. Righteousness comes from Jesus, not from us. We have been made righteous because Jesus' Blood has cleansed us. We pray in the Name of Jesus with God's authority, in agreement with the Blood Covenant, knowing Jesus Christ has made us righteous.

When we understand we are righteous and embrace Christ's power given to us, we'll pray effectively. May the Holy Spirit deepen our understanding of this scripture. God's righteous children release His power and witness miracles, signs, and wonders.

During a mission, on our break day, Bridge for Peace missionaries went out to relax while Ed and I stayed behind. A team of spiritual directors asked me if I would counsel with a woman. I was quite tired and looking forward to some rest. However, I sensed the Lord's will in their request, so I asked the Lord to strengthen me to say yes to Him.

The tall, slim thirty-year-old woman sat with me in a private room. She told me blasphemy constantly ran through her head. She loved the Lord and at one point in her life had begun the process of becoming a nun. She wasn't an irreverent person. She didn't normally speak or think in disrespectful terms, but an evil spirit was plaguing her.

The spirit of blasphemy is not uncommon.   I've often seen this spirit tormenting clergy. This often results in overwhelming feelings of shame.

She had some concerns about her brother in seminary who was suffering with tormenting spirits. I listened. Then I encouraged her to intercede for him and herself praying, "The Word says the prayers of a righteous person are powerful and effective."

"Now the spirit is blaspheming you," she replied.

I entered the session very worn out and I sensed the demon wanted to shock me and engender fear. It seemed the ultimate objective was to get me to back off. However, the tactic had the opposite effect. Righteous anger rose up in me.   I thought, *How dare this demon afflict this dear child of God.*" Holy Spirit power moved through my body, energizing me for battle. I began to minister James 5:16 to her.

The prayers of a righteous person, a person made righteous by the Blood, are powerful and effective. At first she objected, "I don't know that I am righteous." I explained righteous means in right standing with God. Through the Blood of Jesus, disciples have been made righteous.

The woman began to understand her identity had been robbed. The power of the Blood Covenant was ineffective in her because she had no concept of her inheritance. She was being abused by the powers of hell. I watched her expression change as she grasped the revelation of God's empowerment. Understanding spread across her face. She knew she could effectively pray for herself and for others. She could expect good fruit from her prayers.

13) Comment on being made righteous by Christ versus self-righteousness.

_____

_____

Jesus Christ instructed us to speak in the authority of His Name. The Holy Spirit shows us how to pray.

14) Is God asking you to take authority and release His power into a situation right now? Explain.

_____

_____

_____

NOTES

_____

_____

_____

_____

_____

_____

_____

_____

_____

_____

PART TWO

LESSON THREE

HOLY SPIRIT EMPOWERMENT

We study Jesus' instructions about the Holy Spirit and the disciples' Pentecost experience as a basis for discernment, prayer, and self-examination. What place does the Third Person of the Trinity hold in our lives? What is the evidence of Holy Spirit power in us? The Baptism of the Spirit and speaking in tongues is often considered peripheral to belief in Jesus Christ. However, if salvation does more than settle the question of where we spend eternity, if salvation transforms the purpose of life *today*, then the question of Holy Spirit empowerment shifts and becomes a central issue. Our goal is not only eternal life in heaven, but a victorious life on earth. Jesus said the Holy Spirit's dynamic power gives us ability to live the Word. In this lesson, we study Holy Spirit empowerment and ponder the implications of scriptures for our lives, especially as they relate to the healing ministry.

> **Our goal is not only eternal life in heaven, but a victorious life on earth.**

PASSOVER

Through John 16:5-7 we break in on a heartrending moment. The room is prepared for Jesus and His disciples to celebrate Passover– an annual feast instituted the night before God delivered the Israelites from Egyptian captivity. Passover still means families around the table together, remembering sorrows and joys, recalling ancestral struggles, laughter ringing out, and traditional comfort food. In your mind's eye, see the disciples seated around the table with Jesus. He has been acting strange—washing their feet as a servant would, warning them of coming betrayal—His mood is solemn, not celebratory as one would expect.

He tells His disciples He's on the way to the One who sent Him. Jesus says it's better for them if He goes.

1) What reactions do you think the disciples may have had when Jesus said it was better for them if He left?

_____

_____

_____

When Jesus said it would be better for them if He went, it seems natural to me that some may have wondered, *What kind of crazy talk is this? How could it possibly be better?* I imagine Jesus' statement would have been met with resistance. Jesus explains Himself. He outlines why it would be better for them if He went.

2) What reason did Jesus give? (Read John 16:5-7.)

_____

THE HOLY SPIRIT

The coming of The Counselor, The Friend, was conditional on Jesus' leaving. Perhaps the disciples wondered, *What's so important about the coming of The Friend?* Jesus occasionally showed He knew His disciples' thoughts. It's as if He knows their objections now and He begins to tell them *why* they need the Friend.

3) What does Jesus say the Holy Spirit (Whom He names the Friend, Comforter, Counselor, Advocate) will do? (Read John 16:8-15.)

_____

_____

_____

_____

4) Choose one of the functions of the Holy Spirit you identified in the last question. Discuss how the Holy Spirit has moved in your life in that particular way through either conviction of sin, teaching the meaning of righteousness, judgment, etc.

_____

_____

_____

After Jesus spoke, I wonder what the disciples thought about the Friend, Comforter, Counselor, and Advocate?

5) After meditating on Jesus' Words, how do you think Jesus described the Holy Spirit—unimportant, somewhat important, or very important? Share a few thoughts on this topic.

_____

_____

_____

While Ed, Kevin, and myself were on mission in China, we met a slim young man, well over six feet tall, named David, at a local shop. He wanted to practice his English and asked to walk with us as the sun set. As we strolled, we remarked on a kiosk with shelves of lotus flower shaped candles. David said it was customary to make a wish and light a candle. One would set the candle in the river and walk beside it as it floated downstream.

"Why don't you do it?" he asked.

Kevin said, "We're Christians. We don't wish, we pray."

"Okay," David responded. "You pray then."

We purchased the candle and wound through narrow streets to the river. We lit the candle at the water's edge and David shouted, "Okay. You pray now!" Surprised by his bold announcement, I turned to look at him and saw the street filled with Chinese people who had followed us to see what the Americans were doing. We prayed our hearts out for light to come to the Chinese people and for a River of Life to flow in their nation. We released the candle and walked alongside it, keeping the candle in view as it bobbed downstream. Carefully, Kevin and Ed took turns speaking to David about God's Word. We learned David believed in Jesus Christ and he had part of the Bible.

The next day, we were back in town and heard someone behind us call out a greeting. Turning, we saw David catching up to us. We walked together and David said he needed more information about Jesus.

I answered, "We can have a lot of information, but what we need is understanding. The Holy Spirit is the One Who gives us understanding."

"Holy Spirit? What is Holy Spirit?"

We tried to explain. Eventually, David took out his pocket translator and put in Holy Spirit. He said, "Now I understand."

Of course, we had no way of knowing what he understood, because we couldn't read the translation. We told David the Holy Spirit is God and the One who brings supernatural understanding of Jesus. "Do you want to receive the Holy Spirit?" "Yes." Realize, this conversation was potentially dangerous for David and we had to be very careful. We prayed for David beneath the shade trees, and immediately began walking again.

"This is the happiest day of my life," David said in wonder. "Everything looks new," he remarked glancing up at the sky and at the trees lining the pedestrian walkway. "My whole life is changed from this moment." David had personally met The Friend.

6) How have you come to know The Friend? Do you remember a specific meeting?

_____

_____

_____

The disciples witnessed Jesus heal lepers and cripples, and bring dead people back to life. They watched Jesus command demons to leave people's bodies and heard evil spirits scream as they submitted to Him. They listened to Jesus forgive sins. Jesus performed wonders before their eyes. He multiplied loaves of bread and fish, changed water to wine, and told Peter where to find the money when the temple tax was due—in the mouth of a fish! (Matthew 17:24-27)

Scripture records the disciples jubilant because demons submitted to them when they used the Name of Jesus (Luke 10:17). They had personal experience of the power of His Name.

They knew Jesus died by crucifixion and they knew where He was buried (Luke 23:55). A few saw the empty grave after Jesus rose (John 20:1-10). Many saw Him alive again (Luke 24:13-15). Finally, Jesus meets with His disciples to give them last instructions. At this point, the disciples have lived with Jesus, been personally taught by Him, and they have seen demons made subject to them when they used His Name (Luke 10:17).

7) What does the Bible say was the level of their faith? (Read Matthew 28:16-18.)

_____

_____

_____

Doubted in the Greek means "to waver in opinion." Scripture notes their doubt. Though handpicked by Jesus, personally instructed by Him, privileged to ask Him their questions and hear Him explain parables, still some wrestled with doubt. (See Mark 16:11,14; Luke 24:11,41; John 20:24-29.) They were ordinary people, not faith superheroes.

Jesus knew their conviction wavered, but still He told them to go make disciples of all nations. He also told them not to leave Jerusalem. Jesus said He was sending down what the Father promised. He instructed them to stay in the city, not to try to do a thing. They were about to encounter the Holy Spirit and experience a supernatural faith acceleration (Luke 24:49).

8) What event did Jesus tell the disciples to wait for? (Read Acts 1:4-9.)

_____

These men and women didn't read the New Testament, they lived it. They saw Jesus change water to wine. The disciples prayed for the demonized and they were delivered. Peter even walked on water. Yet, Jesus told them not to do anything until they received the Baptism of the Holy Spirit. With all of their incredible experiences, they were not ready to preach, teach, or lay hands on anyone. "Wait," Jesus said.

9) What does Jesus say would happen to His disciples when the Holy Spirit came upon them? (Read Acts 1:8.)

_____

_____

10) In your opinion, how important did Jesus consider the Baptism of the Holy Spirit to be for His disciples? Explain your answer.

_____

_____

_____

PENTECOST

Pentecost (fifty days) in Israelite tradition is also the Feast of Harvest (Exodus 23:16). This joyful Israelite celebration commemorates God's giving Moses the Ten Commandments and includes sacrificing first fruits of the wheat harvest. On Pentecost, the disciples were together in the upper room.

Something sounding like a powerful wind from heaven swept through the building where they waited. Then with their own eyes they saw flame appear in mid-air, it split and hovered over each one! How did they feel? Terrified? Exhilarated? The Bible says they were _all_ filled with the Holy Spirit. Not one was left out.

In addition, they each began to speak foreign languages. The Spirit gave them ability to do this. Many heard their own language spoken and marveled at it. Skeptics ridiculed the disciples. (Read Acts 2:1-13.) We see from this passage that the gift of tongues was controversial from the beginning.

There is more than one form of supernatural tongues. Yes, the disciples spoke in other languages and people of other lands understood them. This type of "tongues" is still in evidence today. People have told me I have spoken Estonian (I didn't even know there was a nation called Estonia at the time), Arabic, Italian, and Hindi. I still remember the lady from Estonia running up the church aisle to me, her eyes filled with tears to hear her own language. The Italian lady was moved when the Lord caused me to say she was the love of His heart in her native tongue. The Arabic translator asked if I spoke Arabic. I did not (as I do not speak any of the other languages). She said I was repeating, "Fire, fire, fire" as I prayed in the Spirit. And a lady recently returned from India told me I spoke Hindi as I prayed in tongues. The Holy Spirit still works through people by the gift of tongues in other languages.

We will confine our discussion to glossalalia, tongues as a prayer language. When we feel we cannot adequately praise God and when we don't know how to pray, glossalalia is a treasure. The Holy Spirit praises and prays through us as we manifest this gift.

God uses even our language limitation to glorify Himself. He gives us an opportunity to surrender our limitation to Him through glossalalia. God turns our inadequacy into a marvelous unlimited experience through the gift of tongues. We run out of words to describe the heights of His glory and the depth of our emotions, but we can pray in tongues and feel we have more accurately expressed the praise and thanksgiving in our hearts.

In healing, the doctor's knowledge is imperfect, our knowledge is restricted, but the Holy Spirit has unlimited supernatural knowledge. I am grateful God has given us the gift of glossalalia in times when I wouldn't otherwise know how to pray.

> **We run out of words to describe the heights of His glory and the depth of our emotions, but we can pray in tongues and feel we have more accurately expressed the praise and thanksgiving in our hearts.**

A lady in a discouraging and potentially dangerous family situation came for prayer during street ministry in New York. She needed wisdom and knowledge. She believed in Jesus and had been walking with Him. I asked, "Have you received the Baptism of the Holy Spirit?"

"No, I haven't. I don't want to play with God if I'm not ready," she said.

"As far as I understand," I said, "God says believers are not ready when they don't have the Holy Spirit. Jesus didn't ask the *apostles* if they were ready to receive the Holy Spirit. Jesus said wait until you receive the Holy Spirit.

"You've received Jesus Christ and now you need Holy Spirit empowerment to walk in all Jesus Christ has shown you. The apostles just had to wait on God to receive the Holy Spirit.

"If you don't have Holy Spirit power in your life, you don't have what Jesus told the disciples they needed before they did anything. How are you going to be able to cope with the difficult family situation without the empowerment of the Holy Spirit? I think calling on the Name of Jesus to be saved, loving God, and desiring to follow Him is the preparation to receive the power of the Holy Spirit and the Baptism of the Holy Spirit.

"But it's up to you. Do you want God the Holy Spirit? Do you need the power of the Holy Spirit?"

She said, "Yes, I want it."

We simply prayed. And the Holy Spirit fell upon her in a new way, as Jesus said. The same thing happened to her as the apostles experienced in Acts. Right there on the street, she received the Holy Spirit. Jesus sent her the Friend, as He said He would.

Once she received the Holy Spirit, she started to speak in the precious gift of tongues. And as she spoke, she smiled and her face became more radiant as she spoke in tongues.

11) In your opinion, what readies us to receive the Baptism of the Holy Spirit?

_____

_____

_____

While ministering in Australia our schedule called for a youth group meeting one afternoon, and a healing service in the same church that night. I asked the youth minister if the young people had been baptized in the Holy Spirit. She said they had not, but felt they were ready. I pointed out scriptures about the Holy Spirit. At the end of the meeting, we baptized all those who chose to receive the Holy Spirit.

Each one who wanted the Spirit received Him. The Baptism of the Holy Spirit is given for action. We invited the teens to serve at the evening healing service and taught them to pray for the sick. They began by ministering to each other.

Sprains and strains were healed as they lay hands on each other. Both the team and the teens were excited to see God's healing power operating through them. Each one they prayed for testified to a healing.

One man misread the schedule and attended the teen service at 4pm instead of the adult service at 7pm. A pair of girls had finished praying for one another. I asked if they'd be willing to pray for the gentleman.

He'd been in a bad motorcycle accident. He'd undergone several surgeries for his foot. He was in constant pain and had weight-bearing problems for twenty years. The girls prayed for him and he was healed! This man, who was a nurse, wrote a four-page testimony explaining his difficulties and proclaiming the healing. He was amazed at the power of God flowing through the two young women.

That evening the teens came and assisted the Bridge for Peace team in praying for those who'd come for healing. They also released the Baptism of the Holy Spirit for anyone who wanted to receive it.

A young man went to one of the Bridge for Peace teams. He was an excellent sportsman, but had been hurt playing cricket. He'd been in physical therapy (or physio, as they say in Australia) for a long time with little relief. The team prayed for him and he was healed.

Later that night, the young man asked me if he could help us pack up. Some of the teams were still praying and I welcomed his help. Then I thought, *Lord, this boy wants something.* I asked him. "Were you here this afternoon?" "No, but my sister was." "Did she receive the Baptism of the Spirit?" "Yes, she did." "Did she receive the gift of tongues?" "Yes." "Do you want that?" "Yes." We sat in the pew and I prayed for him. Next thing, he was speaking in tongues. The young man wrote a testimony about his healing and receiving the gift of tongues saying, "My whole life was changed."

This power of the Holy Spirit is what is needed to make disciples of all nations. The disciples showed a person doesn't have to be super-spiritual to receive the Holy Spirit. The Holy Spirit equips doubters, enlivens faith, deepens understanding, and gives power to carry out God's commission. The disciples didn't become smarter; revelation is supernatural, independent of intellectual ability! God gave them knowledge of His ways. We, too, may grapple with our faith, and still God tells us to go make disciples. We all need the Holy Spirit's touch for a supernatural faith acceleration.

12) Have you received the Baptism of the Holy Spirit?

_____

13) If you haven't been baptized in the Spirit, do you want to be?

_____

You can ask the Holy Spirit to baptize you. Simply ask Jesus to baptize you with the Holy Spirit or ask someone who has been baptized in the Spirit to pray with you. In the next lesson, we suggest a prayer for the Baptism in the Holy Spirit.

PART TWO

LESSON FOUR

THE BLOOD COVENANT PRAYER

In this lesson we familiarize ourselves with the scriptural foundation of the "Blood Covenant Prayer". You can then decide if it is suitable for your use when praying for others. We have found it invaluable to have the "Blood Covenant Prayer" taped into the front of our Bibles to pray with people seeking healing prayer. This scriptural prayer was researched by Vaughan Colebrook from Australia who was miraculously healed of a crippling disability. We thank him and Ellen Colebrook for their teachings and generosity toward Bridge for Peace. We have made minor modifications to the original. Vaughan's scriptural studies and efforts pulled the elements of the prayer together, but I have made the prayer my own.

Ed and I have seen Jesus change lives as we've prayed the Blood Covenant Prayer with people in many different situations. Some want to acknowledge Jesus Christ as their Lord for the first time and some want to recommit their life to Christ. Some want to be baptized in the Spirit, others have loved the Lord but never understood their inheritance in Him. The prayer is helpful for uncovering needs for repentance and helping people to repent. The Blood Covenant Prayer can assist those who struggle with unforgiveness, those who are ready to forgive, and those who need help to forgive.

The Blood Covenant Prayer

Father, I come to You in the Name of Jesus. I recognize that You love me and sent Your Son Jesus to remove my sin that separates me from You.

I respond to Your love and repent of all my sin. Please forgive me and cleanse me by the Blood of Jesus Christ. By faith, Father, I now receive Your forgiveness and cleansing in Jesus' Name. I thank You that Your word says I am now brought near to You because of the Blood of Jesus Christ through which I enter Blood Covenant relationship with You now.

> **I recognize that You love me and sent Your Son Jesus to remove my sin that separates me from You.**

I renounce the lordship of satan over my spirit, soul, (mind, thoughts, will, intellect, emotions) and my body. I renounce every hold or influence of the devil in all areas of my life, including everything inherited through the generations, because the Bible tells me I have a new Father and I only inherit from Him now.
(This is the time to renounce sin – occult activity, unforgiveness, etc.)

Lord Jesus Christ, I invite You to come into my life and I submit totally to You. I ask You to be Lord of my spirit, soul (mind, thoughts, will, intellect, emotions), and my body. By faith, I state sin will no longer have dominion over me, because Your Spirit lives in me. By faith I am saved, delivered, protected, healed, preserved, doing well, prospering, and made whole by the Blood of Jesus Christ.

Lord Jesus, You are the baptizer in the Holy Spirit. I ask You now to baptize me with the Holy Spirit and fire. I believe, by faith, that when the Holy Spirit comes upon me I will receive power and tell people about You everywhere. I believe as I speak the Holy Spirit will give me ability to speak new tongues. I pray in the Name of Jesus Christ. Amen.

EXAMINING THE PRAYER

Father, I come to You in the Name of Jesus. Jesus said He is the Way, the Truth, and the Life. He plainly said no one can come to the Father except through Him (John 14:6).

I recognize that You love me and sent Your Son Jesus to remove my sin that separates me from You. God so loved you that He sent His one and only Son so that you would not perish but have eternal life (John 3:16-21). Sin separates us from God (Isaiah 59:2). Death reigned in humankind until our Savior Jesus came (Romans 5:12-17). Scripture tells us we were alienated, separated from God. Our attitudes were hostile to Him. Christ, through His body of flesh, has reconciled us to His Father (Colossians 1:21-22).

I respond to Your love and repent of all my sin. The Father's love for us caused Him to send Jesus. Jesus asks us to respond to God's love with repentance (Mark 1:14-15). Acts 3:19 warns us to repent and be converted so that our sins may be blotted out. Repent means to be sorry for sin, to ask God's forgiveness. Repent means to turn away from sin and turn toward God. Repentance is the heart-motivated desire to amend our ungodly habits, abhorring our wrongdoing, and embracing God's ways. Luke 3:8a cautions us to bear fruit worthy of repentance. "Bear fruit" means our lives evidence the characteristics of a godly lifestyle and produce an expansion in God's Kingdom on earth.

Please forgive me and cleanse me by the Blood of Jesus Christ. Hebrews 9:22 instructs us on the necessity of the shedding of blood for the release of our guilt from sin. Without shed blood there is no remission of punishment due from sin. God proves His love for us by the fact that while we were still sinners the Messiah died for us (Romans 5:8). 1John 1:7 says the Blood of Jesus cleanses us from all sin.

By faith Father, I now receive Your forgiveness and cleansing in Jesus' Name. Let's look at this sentence in smaller segments. *By faith*...In order to receive from the Lord we have to step out in faith. Faith pleases God and we reap a reward through faith (Hebrews 11:6). *I now receive Your forgiveness*...Scripture says if we confess our sins He will forgive us (1 John 1:9). *...and cleansing...* Hebrews 1:3 says that Jesus accomplished the cleansing of our sins by offering Himself. *...in Jesus' Name.* Jesus said if we ask in His Name, He Himself will grant our request so His Father may be glorified (John 14:14).

I thank You that Your word says I am now brought near to You because of the Blood of Jesus Christ through which I enter Blood Covenant relationship with You now. Ephesians 2:13 tells us the Blood of Jesus brings us near to the Father. Hebrews 13:20-21 says the Blood of Jesus seals the covenant.

I renounce the lordship of satan over my spirit, soul (mind, thoughts, will, intellect, emotions), and my body. Before receiving Christ, we are ensnared by the devil, held captive by him. We are under his lordship. We escape satan by receiving Jesus, rejecting satan, and preferring God's will (2Timothy 2:26).

I renounce every hold or influence of the devil in all areas of my life, including everything inherited through the generations, because the Bible tells me I have a new Father and I only inherit from Him now. The devil is father to people who willfully gratify ungodly desires or demonic cravings (John 8:44). Applying the sowing and reaping principle, we find the hard-hearted leave an inheritance of bondage (Galatians 6:7). All who renounce the devil and his bondage inherited through generations rejoice in Jesus' assertion that satan, the evil ruler of this world, will be expelled (John 12:31). We agree with Romans 6:14, sin shall not exert dominion over us because we are now under grace.

When the Son liberates us, we are unquestionably free (John 8:36). God, who planned to adopt us as His own children, becomes our new Father. He accomplishes this through Jesus Christ (Ephesians 1:5-6). Whoever receives Jesus has the right to become God's child (John 1:12). Ephesians 1:14 states God's children have received an inheritance from Him. God is able to give us what He calls our rightful inheritance (Acts 20:32).

> **When the Son liberates us, we are unquestionably free.**

(This is the time to renounce sin—occult activity, unforgiveness, etc.) At this point in the prayer we help people by naming any sin the Holy Spirit brings to mind and providing opportunity to reject it. At this point we can help people by asking if there is anyone they need to forgive, and supporting them through the process.

Lord Jesus Christ, I invite You to come into my life and I submit totally to You. I ask You to be Lord of my spirit, soul (mind, thoughts, will, intellect, emotions), and my body. At this point, a mature individual invites Jesus into their life and makes a declaration of obedience to Jesus as Lord. When one prays this way, it is through the power of the Holy Spirit. No one can say Jesus is Lord unless influenced by the Holy Spirit (1Corinthians 12:3b).

By faith I am saved, delivered, protected, healed, preserved, doing well, prospering, and made whole by the Blood of Jesus Christ. By faith we make a personal statement of our position. Many Bibles use the word "confess" to define a personal statement of our faith position. The Bible says when we "confess" Jesus is Lord we will be saved (Romans 10:9). The prayer leads us to declare we are "saved" (sozo). Those who receive Him receive the "sozo" promises. The sozo promises include salvation, deliverance, protection and healing as explored in Part 1, Lesson 3, John 3:16-17. We turn from darkness to light and from the power of satan to God, receiving forgiveness for our sins and a place among those consecrated to God (Acts 26:18).

Lord Jesus, You are the baptizer in the Holy Spirit. John the Baptist told the people Jesus was the One who would baptize with the Holy Spirit (Matthew 3:11).

I ask You now to baptize me with the Holy Spirit and fire. Jesus tells us to ask and we will receive (John 14:13-14). We ask to receive the Holy Spirit, third person of the Trinity, and fire (Matthew 3:11, Luke 3:16-17). The apostles received the Holy Spirit Baptism when tongues of fire appeared and settled over each one (Acts 2:3). The appearance of a flame of fire is associated with the Divine Presence (Exodus 3:2). The Greek word *pur* is translated here as *fire*. The original meaning is lightning, a symbol of the swift release of power. Fire symbolizes power, purification, passion, and holy zeal, as well as judgment.

I believe by faith, that when the Holy Spirit comes upon me, I will receive power and tell people about You everywhere. Jesus said we would receive power when the Holy Spirit comes to us personally. Expectant faith believes Christ's followers can have what the disciples received on Pentecost. Jesus commissioned all believers to go and spread the good news. We believe the Holy Spirit will empower us with gifts and boldness to complete our commission (Acts 1:8).

I believe as I speak the Holy Spirit will give me ability to speak new tongues. New tongues is one manifestation of receiving the Holy Spirit (Acts 2:4).

I pray in the Name of Jesus. Praying in the Name of Jesus means we pray with Him, His Name represents all that He is (John 14:13-14).

Amen. Amen means so be it, trustworthy, surely.

1) Choose one of the above paragraphs. Review the referenced scriptures on that topic. Share a new discovery, a challenge, or an affirmation of a long held belief after exploring the Word.

_____

_____

_____

_____

_____

_____

Bridge for Peace Foundation for Healing

POWER FOR HEALING

While we were on mission in the Philippine Islands, a burly ambulance driver came for prayer. Driving in heavy traffic strained his leg and he had constant, extreme pain. On a scale of one to ten, ten being the most intense, he described his pain as nine. He rubbed his leg while sitting in the chair. His wife stood beside him. They feared he would not be able to continue to work. They said it was extremely difficult to get a good job. He loved Jesus and had been baptized as a child, but had not heard of the Baptism of the Holy Spirit. He wanted the baptism, as did his wife. We prayed. They began to speak in tongues. They sensed the Holy Spirit's presence. Joy replaced their anxiety. I asked him how his leg was and his mouth dropped open! He had no pain. He jumped out of the chair and stomped on his left foot, still no pain! He started jumping, no pain!

He had received sozo power—saved, healed, delivered, and provided for by the Blood of Jesus Christ and the Holy Spirit.

2) How important do you feel it is to offer Holy Spirit Baptism to people asking for healing prayer? Why?

_____

_____

_____

POWER FOR EQUIPPING

I have often seen people who pray to receive the Baptism of the Holy Spirit receive the gift of tongues, physical healing, and emotional healing. This is the evidence of the hidden reality—God empowers people through Holy Spirit Baptism.

I prayed the Blood Covenant prayer with a woman in the Philippines who loved the Lord. She had tried to pray for the hospitalized, but when she entered the ward she would begin to cry. Staff asked her to leave, because instead of helping people she made them feel worse. She was frustrated, because she couldn't fulfill her call. She had compassion, but lacked courage, strength, and inner peace to pray for critically ill people.

We prayed together, she received the Holy Spirit in a dramatic way, trembling under God's power. I received an email after our return to the U.S. This woman was praying for the sick, blessing many people and their families.

3) What personal need for Holy Spirit equipping comes to mind when you meditate on your present challenges?

_____

_____

POWER FOR REPENTANCE

To repent means to be sorry for sins we committed and to desire to behave differently. Repentance means to turn away from sin and to God. Remember, we can't see our own sinfulness. God convicts us of sin. Through the power of His Blood and the Holy Spirit, Jesus Christ frees people who have been unable to go forward.

When knowledge of the need for repentance surfaces be encouraged! The Holy Spirit is at work! When we feel sorrow for sin, enthusiastically repent! Realize it is the amazing Holy Spirit speaking to us, showing us our sin. As we grow more sensitive to the Holy Spirit, we grow in holiness. Let's cultivate gratitude for revelation regarding sin and for the remedy of the Blood of Jesus.

In the Blood Covenant Prayer, people are given an opportunity to repent. They may ask if they are to speak out loud or to themselves. Our preference may be for them to repent silently, but there are benefits to verbalizing repentance. While we *never* compel someone to speak, God has shown me verbal expression can create an opportunity to help people. The following examples demonstrate this.

I prayed with a woman to recommit her life to Jesus and receive the Baptism of the Holy Spirit. I asked, "Is there anything you would like to repent of?" "No." The Holy Spirit prompted me to ask, "Horoscopes? Ouija boards?"
"What's wrong with that?" she asked.

Occult activity—fortunetellers, astrology, numerology, tarot cards—is turning to demonic power. Some think it's just for fun and don't realize it's dangerous and sinful. Turning to the demonic for any reason invites serious, even deadly, repercussions.

We talked. She understood and repented out loud of occult activity. Her body began to twist and turn abnormally, and she went through deliverance from demonic spirits. (Involvement in occult can also cause sickness.) All of this happened because she responded out loud.

On other occasions God showed me the importance of verbal repentance. Praying with a young woman, I suggested we pause and give the Holy Spirit time to speak to us about any area where repentance was needed. After a short time she asked me, "Should I say it out loud?"

"This is between you and God, but you can say out loud anything that comes to you if you like."

"I repent of all my sins," she prayed and, as she began to name things, I sensed the Holy Spirit speaking to me.

"Have you confessed these sins before?"

"Yes." She was repenting of things she'd already confessed. She continued to carry the burden of past sins though she'd confessed them. I spoke about the Blood Covenant and forgiveness. At last, through Holy Spirit revelation, she received her inheritance in Jesus Christ and knew God had forgiven her confessed sins. God didn't remember them anymore. She was set free from the plan of the devil, the accuser, who wanted her to remain in a state of self-loathing for past sins, without any way of escape. Thanks be to our deliverer Jesus Christ who provided our way out!

Some shudder at the word repentance. They project feelings of fear and shame into repentance situations. Like the classic picture of a red-cheeked child caught with his hand in the cookie jar, we imagine guilt and embarrassment. In actuality, "bearing the sin" brings guilt and shame. The aftermath of repentance often brings gratitude, relief, new life, freedom, healing, and joy. I am convinced of the benefits of repentance from firsthand experience and from what I've seen happen on the healing line when people repent. I am grateful for those who have helped me and treasure the opportunity to help others be able to own and confess their sin.

4) Can you share a positive repentance experience?

_____

_____

_____

We first learn attitudes toward repentance and forgiveness in our families. In some families, an insult, real or imagined, caused a family rift that caused the families to stop speaking to each other. Hardheartedness can simmer for generations.

Sometimes people apologize to ease their own conscience, and can leave us in a quandary as to what to do with the information. (For instance, this may happen in adultery cases.)

A person caught in wrongdoing might express regret. Regret means "I'm sorry I was caught," while repentance is genuine sorrow for behavior. Some apologies intend to load guilt on others, making them feel *they* are the problem.

Some family role models apologized for everything, took responsibility when they were not to blame, to keep the peace or for other reasons. We may have lived in a home where people refused to accept apologies.

Perhaps you were owed an apology you never received. Many adults have childhood memories of injustice, but no one has ever admitted to it or apologized for it. Early experiences impact the way we think about repentance.

5) What was your family attitude concerning repentance?

_____

_____

_____

6) Are you owed an apology that you know will never be forthcoming? Discuss your perspective.

_____

_____

_____

Only the Holy Spirit can convict us of sinfulness. Awareness of our sinfulness shows the Holy Spirit is working in us. Spend a little time with the Holy Spirit right now.

7) Do you sense God speaking to you about repentance? Record your insights.

_____

_____

_____

_____

We need to repent for any unforgiveness we hold toward others. God asks us to forgive for many reasons. Before we begin this section on forgiveness, ponder the enormous price Jesus paid for our sins. It is unimaginable.   Jesus bore all our sin.   His sacrificial death paved the way. We can now be forgiven. He restored us to heaven, and demonstrated the power of forgiveness.

POWER FOR FORGIVENESS

About 10pm in Australia, our healing service was winding down when I saw a young couple walk in through the side door holding hands. He was tall and slim, she was petite with long dark hair and olive skin. They slid into the third pew, sat close to the aisle and watched Bridge for Peace teams praying. They listened to people testify to miraculous healings.

The young man approached me and said, "My neighbor was here earlier. He knocked on my door and told me, 'You've got to get down to the church and see what's happening.'"

The young man wanted the Baptism of the Holy Spirit. He received the Holy Spirit and the gift of tongues poured from him. His face was beaming.

The young woman remained in her seat. I sensed the Spirit tell me to go to her. Sitting beside her I asked, "Did you see what happened to him?" She nodded. "Did you come for the same thing?" She nodded again. "Have you had an opportunity as an adult to commit your life to Jesus Christ?" "No." "Would you like to?" "Yes." "Do you want to receive the Baptism of the Holy Spirit, like he did?" She nodded. "Would you like to pray together, commit your life to Jesus and receive the Baptism of the Holy Spirit?" "Yes."

I led the prayer, she repeated, "Father, I come to you in the Name of Jesus..." We came to repentance of sin and I asked, "Is there anyone you haven't forgiven?" Her face hardened, she stared at the floor. "There's someone you haven't forgiven?" No response. "Can you forgive that person now?" No response.

My heart dropped; this was very serious. Then the Holy Spirit touched my mind and showed me how to talk to this young woman. The Spirit gave me an inner vision and explained it to me in a flash. In a conversational way, I repeated to her what the Holy Spirit taught me. This is a close approximation of our conversation:

"Some people are deliberately cruel. They intentionally hurt people. They are abusive and enjoy inflicting pain. They might not ask for forgiveness. They might not care if we forgive them. They might not admit they hurt us. They might even blame us for the situation, twisting facts. When they wound us, it is like they shoot a poisonous arrow deep into our heart.

"When the arrow stays there, it poisons our hearts with bitterness, resentment, rage, and other harmful emotions. Allowed to fester, the poison will spread and make us sick. It can affect our minds and bodies. We can become mentally, physically ill.

"You have an arrow in your heart and you are the only one who can remove it. God cannot remove it, because He chose to limit Himself when He gave you free choice. But God has given you the way to remove it—forgiveness. If you forgive them, it doesn't mean what they did was okay. It means you want to get free of it. God wants us to remember Jesus Christ suffered terrible abuse and forgave His abusers. Jesus chose freely.

"Jesus is praying for you now to make a choice, to choose life. He knows what happened. He knows how you feel. He knows it all. God wants you to choose forgiveness, for your own sake and for love of Jesus. You won't have to forgive by yourself; the Holy Spirit will help you. Then the Holy Spirit will clean the wound and begin to heal you. Can you forgive?"

Crying, she shook her head no. My heart swelled with compassion for her. "You don't have to feel like forgiving. They don't have to deserve forgiveness. You only have to make the choice to forgive."

"I don't have to feel it?"

"No. Forgiveness is not a feeling. It's a choice. A choice God hopes you will make for your own sake. A choice the Holy Spirit will help you to make. Will you let God help you? Will you make the choice to forgive and pull that arrow out of your own heart?

She nodded, tears streaming down her face. My heart sang. We prayed the Blood Covenant prayer together. She received the Baptism of the Holy Spirit and her face transformed. She spoke in tongues. Jesus changed her life.

This young woman didn't believe that she could forgive. She didn't want to forgive. Jesus Christ gave her power to choose forgiveness.

In prayer ministry we have the wonderful opportunity to help people forgive. The Holy Spirit is already at work in their hearts if they know they need to forgive someone. Without the presence of the Holy Spirit we encounter absolute self-righteousness, hard heartedness and defensiveness when we suggest someone may need to forgive. Do all you can to persuade people to forgive or they will be caught in the bondage of satan.

In the repentance section, we searched our hearts for apologies never given or rejected. The person who hurt us may be dead. We still need to forgive them. The Holy Spirit helps us to forgive others and helps us forgive ourselves. The Comforter brings peace.

8) Do you need to forgive someone? Explain.

_____

_____

_____

Forgiveness does not imply acceptance of evil behavior. God does not condone evil. We do not accept evil, nor do we ever put ourselves in harm's way of an abusive person. We forgive people knowing their behavior is evil and they may not even care if we forgive them. God asks us to forgive. Jesus taught us to pray "forgive us our sins as we forgive those who sin against us." Holding unforgiveness has serious consequences.

When we refuse to forgive, we sin against God. We need to tell God we are sorry for unforgiveness and turn from unforgiveness through Holy Spirit power. The Holy Spirit guards us from holding grudges, bitterness, resentment, and blame.

We forgive for the sake of Jesus Christ. We forgive for our own sake, so we may be set free. We forgive for the sake of the other, to set them free. Help people forgive. Unforgiveness can make people sick at heart, in the mind, body, and spirit.

9) Can you make the decision to forgive?

_____

_____

The true test of a Christian is being able to pray for our enemies.

10) What did Jesus say concerning our enemies? (Read Luke 6:27-28.)

_____

_____

_____

POWER THROUGH PRAYER

The Blood Covenant prayer is a commitment or recommitment to Jesus Christ and a request to be baptized in the Holy Spirit.   The previous lessons have prepared you to understand this prayer. You have had the opportunity to study the prayer's scriptural basis. Whether in America, Africa, Asia, Europe, South America, or Australia I have seen God transform lives when people are invited to enter into the prayer.

Though God has shown me His transforming power hundreds of times, I am still amazed to see lives changed before my eyes simply because someone asks God to do it. People need prayer and many people want prayer. I have prayed with people among the clothing racks in department stores, in the stacks at libraries, in parking lots, on busses, on the street, in beauty salons and delicatessens. Find a way to offer prayer to people. You are Christ's ambassador.

Pray with people on the phone whenever you can. It is very effective. My mother is eighty-nine years old. Life isn't easy for her. Occasionally, she feels down and doesn't want to get out of bed. She loses her desire to eat and take her medication. When this happens, my brother usually calls me to speak and pray with her. I tell her about different people who are praying for her and then I pray for her. I remember one day when I finished praying she said, "Okay. I think I'll get up and have breakfast now." I have found Holy Spirit power is released when we tell someone we are praying for them.

God's power is at the ready for whatever is needed. The Blood Covenant Prayer provides helpful guidelines for those ministering and those who are in need of prayer. We hope the Blood Covenant Prayer is a help for you.

11) Make some notes about the Blood Covenant Prayer. Have you prayed it for yourself? What happened? Would you like someone to pray it with you? If you are not in a group study, call Bridge for Peace and we would be happy to pray with you.

_____

_____

_____

Foundation for Healing

Part Three

PART THREE

LESSON ONE

FOUR MANIFESTATIONS OF HEALING

Miracles cannot be classified or compared as greater or lesser. I undertake categorizing healings fully aware of the impossibility, aware that God's miracles defy classification. My intention is not to create definitive categories of healing, but to provide a framework within which we, with our limited abilities, can think about miracles. Based on my observations of many miracles, I suggest these "artificial" categories of miracles as an aid to reflection: natural, accelerated healing, irreversible condition reversed over time or instantaneously, and deliverance.

I hope to stir your memory and stimulate your thinking regarding some of the ways you have seen God's healing power manifested. As you jot down answers you create a written record for future reference for God's glory, and your encouragement and edification. I pray this lesson will result in a new alertness to God's miracle working power, increase expectant faith, cause us to minister with authority, and give hope through Jesus Christ.

MIRACLES

When Ed and I ministered in Jamaica, West Indies, we received a delicious gift—one pound of Blue Mountain coffee in a burlap bag which we immediately packed into our suitcase. Imagine for a moment that the bag tore and coffee beans spilled out. I would have gone to the retreat house kitchen, looking for something to contain the beans. If I returned and found the bag intact and full of beans I might have said, "A miracle!" Yet, probably all of us have experienced something similar which doesn't seem unusual. Our skin is cut. We bleed. In a matter of hours or days our skin is intact, our blood is replaced. A miracle. We expect this healing but, nonetheless, it is miraculous.

We recognize God's extraordinary work in what some consider ordinary.

1) In relation to physical healing, how would you define a miracle?

_____

_____

_____

_____

Bridge for Peace teams operate in gifts of physical and emotional healing. Many people have been healed of fears, unforgiveness, nightmares, and other conditions. Inner healing is often accompanied by emotional release. The release may be in the form of tears or laughter. We give thanks and praise to God for these very important healings. Inner healing, a crucial and beautiful gift, is measured by a sense of increased well being, restored relationships, forgiveness, sometimes ability to sleep, etc. These evaluations are mostly subjective. For this reason, I limit the discussion to physical healings that can be objectively measured and observed.

In 1 Corinthians 2:4 Paul says his message and preaching was not with wise persuasive words, but with a demonstration of God's power.

2) What do you think Paul might have meant by a demonstration of power?

_____

_____

_____

It is human to want to succeed. However, God doesn't ask us to determine our effectiveness, but to obey the Spirit's direction. When we follow the Holy Spirit's leading there is a powerful effect. We might judge our attempt to preach the gospel as a total failure, based on apparent results. Yet, all heaven may be applauding that we took the obedient step, because God knows the fruit.

We can be encouraged by the different ways God used people in the scriptures, as in the case of Phillip and the Ethiopian (Acts 8:26-39). God wants to use you in a unique way. Share your stories, not as methods, but to edify yourself and others. With this foundation in mind, respond to the following questions.

3) When have you experienced the effective preaching of the gospel? Share your experience.

_____

_____

_____

4) In your personal experience of sharing the gospel with family, friends, co-workers, when did it seem people were most affected?

_____

_____

_____

Personal need for God's healing power often creates a receptive atmosphere where the good news can be heard. I want to share the gospel with a demonstration of Holy Spirit power. For discussion purposes, I suggest four categories of miraculous physical healing.

These suggested categories are not all-inclusive, but a starting point for study purposes. Four categories:

- **Natural**
- **Accelerated Healing**
- **Irreversible Condition Reversed Over Time**
- **Instantaneous Reversal of a Condition**

Many think a miracle is *exclusively* an instantaneous supernatural reversal of:
a) a condition expected to be healed over time (skin wound, etc.)
b) a deteriorating condition (arthritis, etc.)
c) a medically irreversible condition (paralysis, etc.)
When observing and exploring the miraculous, I conclude that an instantaneous supernatural reversal of a condition is too narrow a definition. As we broaden our experience through course, may the Holy Spirit guide us into a definition for miracle.

PERSEVERANCE

Some despair if they don't experience instantaneous reversal of their condition. Many times seemingly small, but truly amazing, victories are overlooked. I remember a woman whose autistic child often had severe undiagnosed abdominal pain. He was often rushed to the emergency room. After prayer, the child's digestion improved and the traumatic drives to the hospital stopped. The mother expressed her discouragement regarding factors in her son's health. When a team member reminded her there were no more emergency room visits, she was encouraged. We are grateful to have seen other victories in her son's health.

God knows we can become disheartened. Prayer can be hard work. His Word strengthens us to move forward. It is important to stand your ground and persevere in prayer to receive healing (Ephesians 6:14-18). At times, people have been discouraged from praying for others for fear they are holding out false hope.

A Bridge for Peace colleague desired to visit a woman who was dying in the hospital. My colleague's church advised her not to pray for the patient, because the patient's husband was bitter and blamed God for his wife's illness. *What if I pray and she still dies?* Torn between her feelings and the counsel, she asked my input.

I understood the dilemma, but my allegiance is to Jesus and He will be my judge. I won't stand before a church official, or anyone's relative in the end, only before Jesus. He told me to pray for the sick. I do as God has told me, proceed sensitively, and leave the outcome to Him.

If a spouse is blaming God for serious illness, it is an unrighteous attitude. God is our best friend. I am not going to allow unrighteousness to dictate my behavior. The patient was a churchgoer and my colleague felt she would want prayer. My friend decided to visit and pray. Sadly for friends and family left behind, the patient died. She went to her heavenly home and worships God face to face. Though the lady died, her husband's heart was moved by the fact that someone came to pray for his wife. He was very grateful. Touched by the love of Christ through my friend, he had let go of his anger and allowed the Lord to minister to him. My friend persevered and all were blessed.

A healing service was held for couples who could not conceive and "Ranan," our music ministry, was invited to lead worship. The huge church was packed and couples were outside the doors unable to fit in. People were still on line to receive prayer past midnight. The anguish of the women was terrible. The atmosphere was so intense that the clergyman had to take a break, something I had never seen him do. The couples were encouraged to continue to attend the monthly service until they conceived.

The next month, the service was repeated. The pews were only half full. A few couples came to testify they had conceived. The clergyman who had initiated the monthly services was very sad. Shaking his head he asked, "Where are they? They gave up already? Where is faith?"

5) How do you feel about encouraging people in painful circumstances to persevere to receive healing? How do you feel about praying for healing for a life-threatening illness?

_____

_____

In addition to attending a healing service or having a home visit for the purpose of laying on of hands, individuals can pray for themselves for healing. It is also important to thank and praise God for our expected healing.

6) Do you think it is important to encourage the sick to continue to pray for healing? Give your reasons for your answer.

_____

_____

_____

Natural Miracles
God built miracles into our everyday existence when He created us. Man cannot even heal his own skin, but most cuts and bruises disappear through God's miraculous design of our bodies.

7) What natural miracles have you witnessed?

_____

_____

_____

_____

Accelerated Healing Miracles

When we break a bone, we expect it will heal and be usable again. We expect to recover from flu or fever and to be restored to health. We expect a headache to go away. An accelerated healing is health restored sooner than expected by God's power through prayer.

We've prayed for people in casts because of broken bones. Casts have been removed earlier than expected as physicians noted accelerated healing. We can pray to reduce expected recovery periods.

Ed suddenly fell sick with flu. He had heavy congestion and fever. I prayed for him for several hours and he was noticeably eased. The second day he improved again with prayer. In a few days he was totally healed from a flu expected to have a ten day recovery period.

We expect a headache to have a limited life. We expect them to go away eventually. Many people have been healed through prayer from headaches. Headaches have stopped much sooner than expected. Some have been healed from long-standing conditions of repetitive headaches.

8) Have you witnessed miraculous accelerated healing? Explain.

_____

_____

_____

Irreversible Condition Reversed Over Time

We prayed for a young woman with Celiac's disease, a very serious disease of digestion that can lead to eventual death. There is no known cure. She had lost a lot of weight and was extremely ill. She felt better after prayer and tested the healing by eating a bit of food that previously would have resulted in diarrhea. She was able to tolerate the food. When we returned to her area the following year, she looked whole, at normal weight, and gave a beautiful testimony of how she was totally healed!

We prayed for a woman whose eyes were steadily deteriorating. She wore eyeglass with thick lenses. Over a period of months, her eyes improved until she didn't need glasses anymore.

After receiving prayer, people have told us their doctors have reduced and even eliminated medications for depression and other mental illnesses. Though much emotional and psychological healing is subjective, in these instances we have measurable evidence of healing.

A doctor specializing in rheumatology diagnosed my condition as rheumatoid arthritis. He prescribed medication, some of which had undesirable side effects. He switched the medication until we found an anti-inflammatory I could tolerate. I had constant pain, limited function, fatigue, and weakness. I significantly reduced my activities to a manageable level. The doctor said I had an incurable progressive disease. I attended a healing service and felt no change after prayer that night. A few days later, I felt my joints were a bit lighter.   The healing progressed until months later I was totally off all prescription medication and fully functioning again.

9) Have you seen or heard of an irreversible physical condition reversed over a period of time through prayer? Record your story here.

_____

_____

_____

_____

Recently, I prayed with a doctor who had a torn muscle. She said, "I may need surgery." After prayer she felt no physical change, but had an emotional release, and disclosed other difficult circumstances in her life.

Since she felt no physical change, I encouraged her with my own testimony of the healing of rheumatoid arthritis over time. However, I didn't want her to feel it could *only* happen after time. I didn't want her to think she *had* to wait for healing.

My prayer partner continued to encourage me and the doctor by mentioning an occasion when we both had prayed for an associate pastor. He had pneumonia and had been in the hospital. He was struggling to breathe again, but did not want to go to emergency. He had been to a Bridge for Peace healing service and had seen a friend healed. The friend had been prayed over in the evening and overnight his healing manifested. When we prayed with the associate pastor experiencing pneumonia, he felt instantly healed, but thought it couldn't happen until the next day. So, he didn't tell us he was immediately healed, but waited until the next morning to call with the good news. When we told the pastor many people are healed immediately, he said, "So, it can happen right away?"

10) How important do you think it would be to give testimonies of both instantaneous healings and healings over time? Why?

_____

_____

_____

Instantaneous Supernatural Reversal of Conditions
Often we witness instantaneous miracles. When there is no medical explanation for the healing of a physical condition many people will acknowledge supernatural intervention. We have seen God's miracles and give Him all glory. I offer the following testimonies.

AUSTRALIA

Elena fell off a marble step as a young girl, damaged her spine, and spent twenty years in a back brace. She had difficulty sleeping at night because of pain. She came for prayer. The Holy Spirit moved her spine around in some strange gyrations. I knew she was embarrassed, but encouraged her to move with the Holy Spirit. She received God's healing, her pain left. Ten years ago, after that prayer, she gave away her back brace and is still pain-free today.

A year later, Elena tore her Achilles tendon. Her cast was removed and the same night she came to our healing service. She had torn her tendon before and the doctor didn't expect she would be able to move her ankle. She had a lump of scar tissue the doctor said would have to be surgically removed. Elena asked me, "Can I ask our Lord for another miracle?" I could feel the lump of scar tissue in Elena's ankle. As Holy Spirit power moved through her, I felt the lump shrink! God's miracle power healed her and she began to flex her foot! The next day her doctor reprimanded her. "You were supposed to come in to see me as soon as they removed the plaster cast." Elena explained. "They took the cast off yesterday," she answered. "That's impossible. You couldn't have flexibility in your foot," he said. Elena told him she'd been to a healing service and after prayer she could move her foot again. She quoted her doctor as saying, "I've seen other people healed through the power of prayer." Elena received an instantaneous supernatural reversal and her surgery was cancelled.

NEW YORK

On Long Island a lady came to a service with her arm in a sling for a torn rotator cuff. By the end of the service, she'd gotten rid of the sling and was lifting her arm over her head.

NEW YORK

A woman was receiving cortisone shots on a regular basis for inflammation in her ankle. Her doctor advised surgery and said he would no longer be able to give her these regular cortisone shots. She came for healing prayer.

We found she also needed inner healing. She heard the teaching before prayer time. She wanted to receive Jesus as her Lord and be baptized in the Holy Spirit. We prayed the Blood Covenant Prayer together. She began to cry and experienced a tremendous emotional release. She received the Baptism of the Holy Spirit and was wide-eyed when she began speaking in tongues. She began to rest in the Spirit. She'd never seen this before and was frightened. We assured her it was a natural demonstration of God's power. After some time she stood. I asked, "How's the foot?" "I have to take my shoe off to find out. I can never walk flat-footed." She kicked off her shoes and walked around the sanctuary amazed by God.

BRAZIL

Ed prayed for Ferdinand, an adopted eleven-year-old boy. His birth mother had measles while Ferdinand was in her womb. He was born deaf and mute. Ed prayed for him for a moment, God's power manifested, and the boy was hearing. His mother clutched him to herself with joy. Then she pointed to herself and said to him, "Say Mama." In halting sounds he spoke, "Mama." She broke into tears and the congregation exploded with praise. Ferdinand came to a Bridge for Peace conference the following week in Fortaleza, Brazil. He complained that the praise music was too loud!

11) Have you seen or heard of an irreversible condition supernaturally healed instantaneously? Record the story here.

_____

_____

_____

_____

_____

_____

Deliverance

Sometimes, when you don't see a change after prayer on a healing line, demonic oppression may be the root of the sickness. When the Holy Spirit shows us there is demonic activity, we are to drive out the demon. Jesus said all believers are to do this.

Jesus tells the disciples what to expect in Mark 16:17-18. Jesus Christ's life was characterized by Holy Spirit power. He tells us to look forward to the same lifestyle of driving out demons, speaking new tongues, divine protection, and healing.

12) What do you find most challenging about Mark 16:17-18? Are Jesus' words comforting, reassuring, or exciting? Explain. (Read Mark 16:17-18.)

_____

_____

_____

_____

At times, I have met people at services who struggle with lethargy, heaviness, depression, or other maladies. They believe in Jesus Christ as the only Son of God and ask to receive His healing. We pray, but they do not experience change. We then pray the Blood Covenant Prayer. During the prayer, I discover they are involved with a psychic, or reading horoscopes. Horoscope columns proliferate in newspapers and magazines. People who read them are often surprised to find these predictions are classified by the Bible as occult activities. When they repent we frequently see dramatic change occur.

A person may complain of pain in the foot, receive prayer, be totally relieved of foot pain, but then complain of back pain. Pain that moves around from the shoulder to the hip to the head may signal a spirit of infirmity or a spirit of pain. Undiagnosed pain or other conditions also cause us to consider possible demonic activity. We command the dark spirit to go in the Name of Jesus Christ and through God's power the person is often instantaneously delivered of his or her problem.

A tall distinguished looking man with gray hair came for healing prayer. He was a chiropractor and he had a painful debilitating problem with connective tissue in his hands. The doctor's fingers were twisted and there were lumps under his skin. It was a terrible sight.

"What is your condition?" I asked. He gave me a complicated diagnostic name. I'd never heard of the disease. The name had so many syllables, I couldn't even repeat what the doctor had said. "What is it?" I wondered out loud. Herman, my prayer partner, answered, "It's a spirit." I said, "You're right!" How good it is to have a discerning prayer partner! We commanded the demonic spirit to go in the Name of Jesus Christ. The doctor said. "I felt something leave." His fingers were still twisted, but it seemed he was free of the twisting spirit and only needed healing prayer now to restore his hands. We prayed for healing. His fingers relaxed and opened.

I asked the doctor, "What do you think?" He replied, "Very impressive." I laughed to myself. "Impressive" was the last thing I expected to hear him say, but Jesus Christ *is* very impressive. We asked the doctor to testify and he stood before those gathered. He lifted up his healed hands and told his story. This composed stately gentleman began to cry openly. He testified that his disease was genetic. He had seen what had happened to other family members. He said his fingers would have continued to twist until his hands were useless claws. He gave glory to God.

> **Every healing is a miracle, whether it is what we consider "natural" or a total reversal of the natural order.**

13) Have you witnessed a miraculous physical or emotional deliverance? Explain.

_____

_____

_____

Every healing is a miracle, whether it is what we consider "natural" or a total reversal of the natural order. We give glory to God for all healing.

PART THREE

LESSON TWO

QUALIFIED TO MINISTER

Who is qualified to minister healing? To respond to this question we examine scripture and consider current attitudes. Weighing presented evidence, exposing assumptions and cultural biases, fosters progress toward hearing the Holy Spirit more clearly. Healing ministry has intrinsic responsibilities that we will consider in this lesson. I will mention a few practical points of ministry for reflection.

The Holy Spirit decides who is qualified to minister healing. Any attempt to override the Spirit will end in disaster.

Many churches, prayer groups, and home fellowships have developed criteria for their healing ministry deciding who is qualified to minister. In the best cases, these guidelines are developed for the protection of those who come for healing as well as those who pray for them. Think for a moment about who you would consider qualified to minister. What would you like to see in someone who was ministering healing prayer to you? What qualities would help them to win your trust? You would need to have some level of confidence to open yourself to receive from them. What would help you to receive?

1) Who do you consider qualified to minister healing? Explain.

_____

_____

_____

Healing prayer is very personal. It is wise to seek the Lord about who we allow to minister to us, regardless of their qualifications. Spend some time praying and thinking about who you would permit to minister to you.

2) What are your criteria for those who pray for you? From whom would you be willing to receive healing prayer?

_____

_____

_____

Scripture shows Jesus Christ qualifies Christians to heal the sick. He called His disciples to Himself and gave them authority both to drive out demons and heal the sick. (Matthew 10:1)

While ministering in West Africa, our host told me that our Bridge for Peace Team of lay people had turned their world upside down, because only clergy were considered qualified to pray for the sick. When people saw the Lord using the Bridge for Peace team to heal people, they insisted we must be clergy. Actually, though we explained we were not clergy, they found it hard to believe us. We were told in one area we visited that lay Christians were forbidden to pray for the sick.

3) Have you been encouraged as a Christian to pray for the sick? Explain.

_____

_____

_____

Part of our work in Bridge for Peace is to equip others and encourage them in their giftedness, especially in the area of healing. When a person requests prayer for the gift of healing I ask, "Have you received the Holy Spirit?" If they respond affirmatively, I assure them they have the gift of healing. The healing ministry will test our love, patience, humility, faith, compassion, perseverance and other aspects of character. Serving in the healing ministry can help us develop godly virtue if we listen to the Holy Spirit, lay down our agenda, and obey Him.

4) What trials have you experienced through the healing ministry or how might you expect God to test you through the healing ministry?

_____

_____

_____

BEGINNING IN HEALING MINISTRY

People often ask me how to begin in the healing ministry. The Holy Spirit may be stirring a desire in you to start to pray for the sick. Or perhaps you have years of experience, have seen many of God's signs and wonders, and desire to train others or build a healing team. In Bridge for Peace we have found these steps helpful when you feel called to begin.

The inexperienced desiring to lay hands on the sick may feel understandably awkward and unsure how to begin. Training can help us come into the ease of the Spirit's flow.

To join a Bridge for Peace healing team, we might ask you to come to a service, sit in the front row, observe a team ministering, and pray for the person in need. Everyone is invited to minister by praying in their seats for people in need.

You might then come to several different venues where Bridge for Peace is praying for people. After attending Bridge for Peace healing services, praying in your seat and observing the laying on of hands, we might ask you to join with a team, agree with them in prayer, and observe. You would closely watch the team.

The team leader might ask you to observe and agree in prayer, but not to lay on hands. We do not want to overwhelm a person by having several people lay hands on them. We prefer no more than two people lay hands on someone. When the team leader sees your ability to respect his/her direction, you may be asked to pray verbally as the Holy Spirit leads you.

Ed and I learned in the same way, by observing people who operated in the gift of healing, reading and discussing the Word as it pertains to healing. This is how Jesus trained His disciples; we find He continues to train in this manner. When questions arise from a field situation, we seek the Lord's answers together and counsel each other through the Word.

If you feel called to lay hands on the sick, I encourage you to pray for family members and friends in need, laying hands on them. If you continue to feel called to serve in healing, you might ask the Holy Spirit to guide you to a healing team or mentors.

5) We are all being trained by the Holy Spirit, no matter how comfortable or uncomfortable we feel in praying for the sick. Do you have a sense of where the Holy Spirit is challenging you now in terms of praying for others? Explain.

_____

_____

_____

HOLY SPIRIT QUALIFICATIONS FOR MINISTRY

While on mission, the Bridge for Peace Team trained people in healing using the pattern I detailed above. Our hosts raised a question about the trainees' qualifications.

By human appearance, some of the trainees dressed "differently," but they were modestly attired, so we had no problem with their appearance. Some trainees had concepts that seemed unusual. We may have disagreed with some of their practices or "ways" of ministering to the sick. However, I found each trainee teachable, not asserting his or her own viewpoint, but willing to stand in agreement in prayer and ask questions later. Some trainees were encouraged by the prayer team leader to verbally express their prayer, while the leader stood by to agree and help when needed. If the trainee moved into unacceptable territory, the prayer team leader took the lead and the trainee submitted to the prayer team leader. It is not always easy progressing this way, but I felt all was in order.

Our hosts set the venues and keenly felt their responsibility to the people at the meetings. They were concerned, feeling some of the trainees should not minister and that they as leaders should be the only ones to pray over others.

This was an extremely painful situation for me. While one could say their concern was logical, I felt saddened by the sense of exclusiveness and I feared grieving the Holy Spirit. I sensed the Holy Spirit wanted these trainees to be raised up in praying for the sick. I was certain that the trainees were God's pick, His choice, and I dared not interfere with the Holy Spirit. If I did, I knew He would leave us to choose who we thought looked and sounded "acceptable" enough to minister by human standards. I would not, could not, risk hurting the Holy Spirit to win the approval of our dear hosts who were so kind to us. The Word says, "Do not quench the Holy Spirit." (1 Thessalonians 5:19) Time showed that a spirit of domination ruled in the host group. I was grateful the Holy Spirit had kept me from submitting to it.

Biblical history shows the Holy Spirit is very sensitive and will not remain where human beings insist on controlling things. If we allow the Holy Spirit to order things, He will give us discernment, caution us, and warn us. Healing is the Holy Spirit's ministry and we will lose His glorious Presence if we try to manipulate the healing ministry. The Holy Spirit will fiercely protect the purity of His ministry by affirming and correcting us, instructing us, and urging us to believe for greater things. Our work is to listen and submit.

We must remember, when raising up others in healing ministry, there was nothing attractive about Jesus Christ, nothing to cause anyone to take a second look. There was nothing about His appearance to attract a following (Isaiah 53:2b). The high priests, religious scholars and leaders tried to intimidate Jesus and to disqualify Him from ministering (Luke 20:2).

The prophet Samuel almost fell into the trap of rejecting God's choice when he assessed David's ability by his appearance. (Read 1 Samuel 16, specifically noting verse 7.) The same struggle continues today. I want to find myself on God's side.

6) Have you ever struggled with the way people or things appeared and the Holy Spirit's guidance in the situation? Include any tendencies to disqualify yourself based on self-assessed appearance, inside or out.

_____

_____

_____

GIFTS OF HEALING
Sometimes people ask me if they have the gift of healing. They sense God telling them they will be used in healing. I always encourage people to serve God and others through the gift of healing. The Word says that the Spirit gives gifts of healing to disciples of Jesus (1Corinthians12:4-11).

Compassion, perseverance, and faith are necessary for the laying on of hands to see the sick recover. To minister to the sick, a gift of love is needed. Without love, we are nothing. Without love, there will not be any permanent fruit of the Spirit. People either submit to God and allow Him to develop virtue within or they draw back from the healing ministry. Submission to the Holy Spirit in each other is also crucial. The following stories address the importance of both love and submission.

SUBMISSION

In February, 2006, Mark came to Ciao Roma—a Bridge for Peace fundraiser for our Rome mission. He heard Bridge for Peace was going to Uganda in April. Mark felt his heart race. He had been on mission before, but never to Africa. He had wanted to go to Africa for some time, but hadn't had an opportunity. That night, Mark asked Ed if he could come along to help carry bags or whatever was necessary. Ed and I sought the Lord and God told us through several scriptures that Mark was "holy unto Me." When we heard from the Lord, we had total confidence that Mark was God's pick for the team. We welcomed Mark to join the mission. Mark was paired with a female team prayer leader much younger than him. As Mark was praying, she felt they best not take the prayer in the direction he was going and expressed caution. Mark, who had a lot of experience, had a decision to make. He told us later he thought his prayer partner was a *young whippersnapper.*" After all, who was she to tell him how to pray? However, Mark decided to submit and the prayer was redirected.

That same morning, they prayed for Hilda, a woman who had been lying on a mat for eighteen years with excruciating pain, unable to walk. After prayer, she stood up healed and danced out of the healing rooms and climbed the tree branch steps to the platform. Everyone who knew her was amazed. Mark says if he had not submitted, he wonders what would have happened.   The result may have been discord and resentment. Would Hilda and others have been healed?

7) What is it like for you to submit to someone in authority? Explain.

_____

_____

_____

LOVE

Galatians 5 discusses the fruit of the Spirit. People sometimes judge the "fruit" of ministry by how many people were seen to be healed. But God calls fruit of the Spirit's Presence love, joy, peace, patience, kindness, goodness, faithfulness, gentleness (described as meekness and humility), and self-control. God produces this fruit in us as we serve on the healing team. Love is the first mentioned, and the greatest gift (1 Corinthians13). God's Presence within us begins with love and develops unconditional love. When we serve with love, God is glorified.

Violet lived in a nursing home and needed knee surgery for a very painful condition. Her heart was a concern and the doctors would not operate because of her circulation problem. Her terribly swollen legs looked wooden. She wore elastic stockings on both ankles. The nurse who accompanied her said Violet had dementia. My partner and I began to pray for Violet. I asked her permission and we placed our hands on her ankles. After some time the swelling reduced and the elastic stockings slid down her legs and lay bunched up around her feet!
I asked Violet, "How are your legs?"
She answered me, "My legs don't bother me. It's my knees."
"Okay. How are your knees?"
Violet began to pound on her knees. "The pain is all gone! No pain! No more pain!"
"Well, come on. Let's take a walk," I said.

Violet started to walk, leaving her cane in the pew. "I don't need my cane. Look, I can walk, I can walk!" She started to walk around the perimeter of the whole church. The people cheered for Jesus Christ. Everyone could see the miraculous manifestation. We talked as we walked and Violet was coherent. She looked up in the air and thanked Jesus. When we returned to the front of the church Violet said, "I can dance!"

"Okay, Violet! Let's dance!"

"I don't know how!"

The joy of the Lord was evident in her. She felt such joy in her spirit that she felt she could dance.

The next night Desiree, who had partnered with me, arrived to serve on the team. She said, "What happened last night was amazing. It was one of the most amazing things I've ever seen in my life." I agreed, "It was absolutely amazing what God did!"

She said, "No, Annette. You don't understand. I don't mean the swelling going down. I don't mean the pain leaving her legs. I don't mean the fact that she didn't need her cane anymore. Or that the dementia seemed to be gone. I don't mean any of those things. I mean the love in the ministry." What moved her heart was not the miracle, but the love poured out for Violet.

If the ministry of healing is not carried out with love and humility, then what are the motivations to serve? Galatians 5:26 says, "Let us not become vainglorious and self-conceited, competitive and challenging, provoking and irritating to one another." Without God's anointing, negative characteristics will appear quickly in the healing ministry. I want to state the obvious: in the healing ministry we deal with people who are sick. Some feel unwell or suffer pain which can make them irritable and abrupt. Some have tried everything and are in despair. They come for prayer because there is nothing left to try. Other people with illness do not feel any symptoms, but their anxiety over their condition or medication they are taking causes personality changes. We often minister to people who are frightened, frustrated, and at their wit's end. These are people who need compassion, mercy, and love. If people are in healing ministry for their own glory or for self-centered or competitive reasons, for reasons of envy or jealousy, they will be eliminated because they will not gratify their egos through healing ministry. A vibrant healing ministry is characterized by increasing fruit in the ministers—love, patience, and joy (Galatians 5).

8) Have you ever companioned a sick person in prayer or otherwise? What was the experience like? What was the ultimate impact on your spirit? Is there anything you would hope to do differently if the occasion arises?

_____

_____

_____

_____

_____

_____

ABUSES

God is not pleased if we do damage to His Body through the healing ministry. We must never judge or condemn. At times, desperately sick people are told they are not healed because they do not have faith, or they have "hidden sin". The sick person then desperately tries to uncover the "hidden sin". They worry, "How do I get more faith?" If a sick person comes looking for the release of the power of the Blood of Jesus Christ and walks away condemned, we have served neither God nor the person in need.

I've often encountered the following scenario. A woman asks for prayer for emotional healing. She says she's been sexually abused, but has no memory of it. I ask, "How do you know that happened?" She replies, "Someone prayed over me last week and told me they "sensed" sexual abuse was the root of my problem." I have met people who have been tormented for years by something spoken to them when they came for healing.

In my experience, God's prophetic word or the Holy Spirit word of knowledge comes to bring healing or conviction through correction. Words in the example above bring grief, fear, desperation, and terror. God's word comes with the power of liberation. If someone walks away with a worse problem than they came with, it is spiritual abuse. By the Blood of Jesus I pray for the healing of those who have been spiritually abused.

9) Have you had a negative experience when seeking help through prayer? Explain.

_____

_____

_____

SOME RESPONSIBILITIES WHEN MINISTERING HEALING PRAYER

Bridge for Peace typically prays for healing after a scriptural message and team testimonies. For example, perhaps the message has been, "Extraordinary God in an Ordinary World." When I begin to pray for the sick after the message, I incorporate words from the teaching as much as possible. I might pray, "God you are extraordinary, this sickness is ordinary. I release Your extraordinary power for the healing of this ordinary illness." Bridge for Peace teams have found during prayer ministry that speaking the Word that resonates with them from the message often results in a rapid visible manifestation of God's Presence. The Spirit may display His power in shaking, trembling, in the sensation of heat or cold! If there is no message and God has spoken to you in your personal prayer time, use the word God gave you, scriptural or personal, as the Spirit leads.

On a healing line we never want to "lead" a person's answer. Ask, "Is there any change?" rather than say "It looks like there is more flexibility in your foot." Most people who come for healing are sincere seekers. They want to see the healing power of God in their lives. Sometimes people say their problem has improved because they feel sorry for the healing minister who has been praying so long. We want to be sure people give an honest assessment of their situation and own the change so God will be glorified.

I recently visited a God-believing elderly man in the hospital at his daughter's request. He had fallen and that precipitated a long hospital stay involving surgery, pneumonia, etc. I prayed with him for awhile and he said, "You'd better go home now. You've been praying for so long. You must be tired. You'd better go home." His wife and daughter were there. We all smiled and reassured him, explaining I was happy to pray with him. You may come across this same objection when praying for people on the healing line.

It is not uncommon for those who come for healing to apologize for taking too much of the prayer minister's time. We reply that God wants to minister to them, it is our pleasure to serve God and them in the ministry, and we're not concerned about the time.

We want people to be able to give a testimony to glorify God. Encourage people to believe and receive, then persevere as the Holy Spirit leads. Remember, there is a right time to *end* the prayer. It is our responsibility to continually develop sensitivity to know when the Spirit is leading you to end. As you learn to obey God in the proper time to finish prayer, you acknowledge healing is about His power not the length of the prayer. In so doing, you will not exhaust yourself or weary those who come for prayer.

In the healing ministry we let the person's doctor give the evidence. We never tell people they are healed, they tell us. We never counsel about diet, medication, exercise, or other medical concerns. Actually, we never counsel at all. Our responsibility is to release the power of the Blood of Jesus.

10) We have explored scripture as it relates to ministers of healing and a few practical points. What have you heard the Holy Spirit saying as you've studied? Does the Spirit's voice affirm or challenge your perceptions of either your own personal qualifications or others' qualifications to minister? Explain.

_____

_____

_____

PART THREE

LESSON THREE

WHEN YOU DON'T SEE HEALING

As students seeking Holy Spirit guidance we begin to examine the question, "Why don't we see everyone healed?" Those in healing ministry and those seeking healing eventually grapple with this question. When a loved one dies, some struggle with this question. Hurting people may ask you this question. Approach this lesson with reverence. Begin with prayer, humility, and a teachable spirit. Ask the Holy Spirit to give understanding and revelation.

We will study related scripture and examine spiritual laws. I offer examples of attitudes observed in real life to assist our study. Hopefully, these seemingly contrary true stories will stimulate prayerful discussion and study. We know healing depends on God, not on us. Our goal as we study scripture is to help people choose to receive healing, never to condemn them.

DEATH
Death brings pain to the survivors and changes lives forever. Approach the subject with tenderness and compassion. We are not dealing in abstracts, but with human suffering.

Think of our Lord. Jesus Christ died at 33, what we would call an early death. Think of His mother, His friends. We might think Christ died prematurely, but His death, as His life, was in perfect rhythm with His Father's will. There is an appointed time for us to die. Remember, God's original plan for us was paradise, or what I call Plan A. Life in a fallen world and death was not God's choice for us. We're all living Plan B (Genesis 3:22, Psalm 90:10).

The consequences of humankind's rejection of God include mourning the death of those we love, and sometimes of strangers, when worldwide tragedies touch our lives. As you pray for the critically ill and the medically hopeless you will see miracles and you will have the privilege of ushering some to the edge of new life in heaven. The very elderly, who are about to meet God face to face, also need prayers for a peaceful death.

When we pray for the critically ill to be healed and they die, reactions differ. Some respond with strong feelings, others go numb. Some enter into a deeper relationship with God, others look to place blame. Blame can be directed at God, themselves, the family, medical staff, or the person who died. I have seen people who don't work through their experience either slowly drift away or abruptly turn from God.

1) Have you ever prayed with faith for someone to be healed, but the person died? Explain.

_____

_____

2) How did you feel?

_____

_____

3) How do you feel about it now? What helped/hindered you when grappling with the situation? Have you sensed any peace regarding the experience? Explain.

_____

_____

_____

Whenever we pray for someone who dies it is good to ask the Holy Spirit, the Comforter, to minister to us and receive healing. The Holy Spirit waits for our invitation.

CALLED TO HELP

Sometimes, when we don't see healing, there is a tendency to blame people. I have heard people say, "She isn't healed because she doesn't have enough faith." Or, "I sense he has held onto unforgiveness, that's why he's not healed."

> **Read scripture to discover ways to help people, not to judge them.**

It is a big mistake to casually dismiss a person who is not healed. It is a big mistake to believe we are experts and imagine we know the reason. We are disciples, followers, trainees. When God expressly reveals information to us concerning another, receive it humbly. If God gives supernatural understanding of a heart matter, we are to help the person come free, not condemn them. Read scripture to discover ways to help people, not to judge them.

Never casually discuss people's situations either within a healing team or with anyone else. The healing ministry is a sacred trust; never treat it as ordinary. Remember the price Jesus paid for each of us. God's extraordinary love makes each one of us His central concern.

There are times and places to rightly discuss situations on the healing line both to learn and to teach. It is appropriate to share various healing situations for additional prayer for the person or yourself, for increased understanding for yourself and those in prayer ministry, or to give glory to God.

4) Where do you share your experiences of healing in the Name of Jesus? Are you accepted there? Is it a place where you can grow? Are your needs to freely explore met in that place? Do you need to consider changes or do you need to put a support system into place?

_____

_____

_____

UNFORGIVENESS

A friend's daughter died in a car accident.   She refused to forgive the other driver and was consumed with the desire to see him in jail. She became increasingly bitter and vengeful. Her body began to swell and she appeared pregnant. Her condition could not be diagnosed. She was hospitalized. She remained undiagnosed and grew sicker. She died in the hospital.

We may encounter a person who is unwilling to forgive. I have observed in myself and others that unforgiveness hinders healing. I know if I refuse to forgive someone, I cannot be healed. If I hold onto resentment, it grows. Our work is to forgive and help others reach a point where they can forgive, not to judge them.

> **If God gives us a supernatural understanding of a heart matter, we are to help the person come free, not to condemn them.**

5) What might you do to help someone who says they cannot forgive?

_____

_____

FAITH

When we don't see healing, sometimes people blame it on faith. Study the following scriptures and think about faith's impact on healing.

6) What did Jesus do in John 11:43-44? (Read John 11:1-51.)

_____

_____

_____

7) Did Lazarus' resurrection depend on his faith? Explain your answer.

_____

_____

8) What about the other people in this example? What did they do? Did they have faith for Lazarus' resurrection?

_____

_____

9) What role did faith play?

_____

_____

10) What did Jesus do when he visited Nazareth, His hometown? (Read Mark 6:1-6, Matthew 13:54-58.)

_____

_____

11) What did the people of Nazareth say?

_____

_____

12) What was their faith response?

_____

_____

13) What did Jesus say?

_____

_____

14) The Bible describes Jesus' feelings in Mark 6:6. What does it say?

_____

_____

15) What role did faith play?

_____

16) Who was Jairus? (Read Mark 5:21-42.)

_____

_____

17) What did Jairus ask and what does this say about his faith?

_____

_____

18) What did the messengers say? What does this say about their faith? (Read v.35.)

_____

_____

19) How did Jesus respond to the messengers?

_____

_____

20) How do you feel about Jesus' response to the messengers?

_____

_____

21) What two things did Jesus ask of Jairus?

a)_____

b)_____

22) What did the crowd do? (Read v.38-40.)

_____

_____

23) Who did Jesus allow to be present, who did He dismiss, and why might He have done this?

_____

_____

_____

24) What do the parents' actions say about faith?

_____

25) Did the daughter's miracle depend on her faith?

_____

26) What do these verses say to you about faith and healing?

_____

_____

27) What did the disciples try to do in Mark 9:14-29? (Read also Matthew 17:14-21, Luke 9:37-43.)

_____

_____

_____

28) What did Jesus say?

_____

_____

Lazarus was dead, but came out of the grave when Jesus called in a loud voice, "Lazarus, come out!" Lazarus' "healing" didn't depend on his faith. He was dead. Yet, Mark 6:5 says Jesus could not do any miracles because of lack of faith, except lay His hands on a few sick people and heal them. In this scripture, God shows us the importance of faith. Their little faith limited what Jesus could do. We come back to what we studied in the Old Testament, our omnipotent God Who for a time has chosen to limit Himself. These examples concerning the importance of faith in miracles invite deeper study and prayer for Holy Spirit understanding.

29) What do you notice in these examples about the necessity of faith in the healing ministry?

_____

_____

PERSEVERANCE IN PRAYER

Sometimes people feel failure and shame when they are not totally healed at once, as if it is their fault. Actually, they may need more prayer. Sometimes people feel shame to ask for more prayer if they have some symptoms return. In Bridge for Peace we'll pray with people for healing as long as they are willing to persevere.

A woman suffering with painful spasms in her neck and a clenched jaw received freedom one night at a healing service. A month later she returned. She was much improved, but was experiencing some symptoms again. She felt ashamed. She told me she was reading a magazine article, "The Twelve Reasons Why God Doesn't Heal Us." She was trying to figure out what she did wrong.

I believe it is better to read the scriptural word, study "Jesus the Solution" and the healing Word of God, rather than study "Why God Doesn't Heal Us". The Holy Spirit will reveal to sincere seekers anything in our spirits that needs to be addressed.

30) Why might someone feel shame when asking for prayer for their symptoms? How might you encourage them?

_____

_____

31) What happened in Mark 8:22-25?

_____

_____

32) How did Jesus react to the blind man's statement that he was not totally healed?

_____

_____

33) How would you apply Jesus' example to how you pray for the sick?

_____

_____

_____

_____

RECEIVING JESUS CHRIST AS SAVIOR

Some say people aren't healed because they haven't received Jesus Christ as their Savior. Yet, we have seen God heal unbelieving people who have then responded by believing Jesus Christ is the Messiah. God repeatedly demonstrates this in the Bible. Healing becomes a way to evangelize.

A Hindu lady, a doctor, came to a meeting we held to teach people how to pray for the sick. She had been in a bicycle accident as a child in India. She sat down and pulled up her trouser leg to show me the result. Her leg looked like a broomstick. It had little muscle. She removed her shoe and showed me her twisted foot. I asked her if she wanted to know Jesus as her Savior. She refused the invitation. We felt God wanted us to pray for her to see a miraculous healing. My partner said, "God's going to do this for you *anyway*." Ladies gathered around her laying hands on her shoulders. I knelt on the floor, my hands on her twisted foot. The Holy Spirit would allow me to say only two words, "Total restoration." Over and over I repeated the same two words. She started crying profusely. I repeated "total restoration" for about twenty five minutes while we watched her foot untwist before our eyes! Again, we asked if she would like to serve Jesus Christ as her Lord. "Yes," she cried. However, she said it wasn't because of the miraculous healing of her foot. She wanted Jesus as her Savior because the love she felt flowing from the ladies was a love she had never felt in her life! It was the love of Christ moving through the ladies that drew her to God! (It really was *total* restoration!)

A lady was brought to a Bridge for Peace healing team. She had pain and restriction in her neck. The friend who brought her described her as "a great intercessor". The team prayed with her with no visible or felt results at all. I was sitting in the pew, observing. I suggested the Blood Covenant Prayer. The team asked the lady if they could pray together restating faith in Jesus Christ as Savior. She refused, turned away, and walked out of the church.

34) A Hindu lady who did not want to receive Jesus Christ received a miraculous healing. Another lady, known as a Christian and a "great intercessor", experienced no change and refused to pray the Blood Covenant Prayer with the team. What are your thoughts about these two situations?

_____

_____

_____

_____

Throughout this course we hear how very careful we must be not to judge. Study the Word, ask the Holy Spirit for understanding and discernment. As we seek the Spirit, God will teach us and give revelation when we are ready to receive it.

SKEPTICISM

Bridge for Peace offers resources at most of our services, including cards to send to the sick. We call them healing cards. These beautiful cards have a message that says Bridge for Peace is praying with faith for the recipient. The sender gives Bridge for Peace the name of the sick person and then mails the card to a friend or relative in need.

A lady came to a healing service and noticed our prayer cards on the resource table. She felt they were beautiful and would be a blessing for her friends. "Is it all right if I take several of them?" She was very positive and affirming about God's healing touch. Yet, when Ed showed slides of miracles we personally experienced, the same lady raised her hand and asked, "What if you are skeptical?" I sensed she asked the question honestly, desiring healing.

She came up for prayer, experiencing tremendous sciatica pain. God instantly healed her. A self-proclaimed skeptic, she was overwhelmed. She looked stunned and said, "I think I have to go home now." She grabbed her coat, pulling it on as she immediately flew out the door of the hall. A lady who attended the same church told us years later the "skeptic" continued to have freedom from sciatica pain. Her "skepticism" didn't hinder her healing.

GENERATIONAL CURSES

During one mission God instructed us to hammer the spirit of suicide. Scores of people came for prayer. Often someone of a former generation had committed suicide and the effects were felt down to succeeding generations, continuing to disturb families. We prayed for the release of the families from their inheritance of grief and for the families to receive their supernatural inheritance of blessings from the cross of Jesus Christ.

FEAR

Job said the very thing he feared had come upon him. Fear can play a role in illness and in our receptivity toward healing. Some believe healing is for others but fear it is not for them. Some cannot hear God's Word through their fear.

I have prayed with many people who were totally healed before witnesses but were in the grip of fear and truly could not own their healing. Though they were healed, they continued to express the hope that one day they would be better. I and others on Bridge for Peace healing teams have witnessed bones straightened out, muscles released and flexibility restored, rotator cuff problems resolved, and yet the persons God touched have had surgery anyway. They said they feared not having the surgery.

Bridge for Peace held a service in a major city. A lady with a severe knee problem attended. Her knee was totally restored. She walked up and down steps without a problem and declared it "miraculous." However, she didn't celebrate her healing. "What will I tell the doctor?" she worried. "I came to this city for knee replacement surgery and the operation is scheduled for tomorrow."

And yet, the power of God is greater than fear. One night a terrified woman came for prayer, literally trembling with fear. She received a miraculous healing on the spot.

EXALTING SUFFERING

Ed and I were asked to go to a meeting to pray for a lady who was wheelchair-bound. (Sometimes people want you to pray for others without considering their friend's desires. People don't always want prayer.) The lady and her pastor were co-leaders of a prayer meeting and they were also the healing team.

Our mutual friend, Terri, brought us to the lady in the wheelchair and introduced us. Terri so much wanted her friend C to be healed. She told C we would pray for her. C said yes, we could pray. C's attitude was odd, almost defiant, as in "I dare you." We know healing belongs to God, not us. And so we prayed.

It then became obvious that C exalted her suffering. She seemed to think her suffering made her holier than others. She thought she was especially chosen to suffer. Her pastor explained. He said, "We believe she is in a wheelchair and suffering with all of these different maladies because she is suffering for God and for (a group of people I won't name)." She was experiencing diabetes and early signs of dementia among other things and was only in her fifties. "We feel God has chosen her for these particular sufferings." If a person believes her disease is a holy gift from God she might have difficulty in receiving healing through the power of the Blood.

When we were on mission in the Philippine Islands there were groups of penitents who volunteered to march down the road, be beaten by those lining the road, and crucified to atone for their sins. (Not crucified to death, but for a period of suffering.) We were repulsed to hear this was an annual event before Easter. Our Philippine hostess considered the participants involved exceptionally holy to subject themselves to this treatment.

We serve a good God, wonderful and generous. Jesus Christ suffered once for all mankind. If we believe that we have to suffer bodily sickness for Jesus Christ and embrace that mindset, then it makes sense to beat ourselves and to be crucified as is the practice of some penitents in the Philippine Islands.

35) What thoughts have you had concerning these topics of skepticism, generational curses, fear, and the exaltation of suffering?

_____

_____

_____

_____

May this lesson be an encouragement to you to seek out godly revelation through prayer and the Word of God to increase your understanding and answer questions you have concerning the healing gift.

PART THREE

LESSON FOUR

GREATER THINGS

Jesus Christ told us to expect "greater things" (John 14:12). This course concludes with an exploration of what "greater things" means to you, personally. Pray for Holy Spirit guidance to expose resistance to receiving and living the full life God desires for you. Spiritual principles are presented from scripture that can help lead you to "greater things".

While keenly aware of today's difficulties, God's grace causes me to maintain a sense of privilege. I see God's awesome Presence in our extraordinary age. God urges me not to be blinded by satan, but to look past the forces of evil to see God's hand at work. We live in a blessed time of history. We live what others may not even have imagined, because our Messiah has come and the Holy Spirit abides with us.

GREATER THINGS

Jesus says in John 14:12, "I tell you the truth, anyone who has faith in Me will do what I am doing, He will do even greater things than these because I am going to the Father."
Jesus' statement invites us to pause and consider His ministry.

1) According to scripture, what has Jesus been doing?

_____

_____

_____

When we describe what Jesus has done we are amazed to realize He can use us to do the same things, including ministering God's healing to others. The word Jesus used, translated as "greater", also means larger, more. As we move in Holy Spirit baptized communities we serve others through God's miracles, signs, and wonders. "Greater" may mean what God does when more believers serve Him. "Greater" may refer to numbers of miracles. "Greater" may indicate that humankind will be astonished by different kinds of miracles God performs through the Body Ministry—a group of present-day disciples ministering together through the power of the Holy Spirit under the headship of Jesus Christ. "Greater" implies something more than the amazing things we've read about Jesus doing in the Bible.

2) What does the phrase "greater things" mean to you?

_____

To participate in God's greater things we need to follow Him. I remember the "What Would Jesus Do?" phenomenon. The question was popular years ago. People wore bracelets, buttons, and knapsacks asking, "What Would Jesus Do?" The slogan counseled people who were uncertain of the right response to pause and ask, "What would Jesus do?" After discerning what Jesus would do, then follow in His footsteps, do the same thing.

3) Discuss an occasion when you experienced an extraordinary result by doing what you thought Jesus would do.

_____

_____

_____

BODY MINISTRY

Jesus said we are going to do these same things He did and even greater things. One way God accomplishes greater things through us is by Body Ministry.

With Christ as our head, all who have received Him become one Body (Ephesians 1:22). God unites many people together, uniting us in His purpose. Prayer groups demonstrate the Body Ministry at work. The Holy Spirit may impress two people to read the same scripture. Two or more may be impressed by the Holy Spirit to sing the same song, speak the same word of encouragement to the assembly, or go to the same nation. In prayer ministry, when two or more have the same impression of how to pray, asking for the exact same thing in Jesus' name, the Body Ministry is at work. I see the Holy Spirit's network functioning in amazing ways every day.

> **One way God accomplishes greater things through us is by Body Ministry.**

While I'm writing this, I'm sitting on a beautiful daybed, an example of God's network. Ed and I have just moved into our home and my 89-year-old mother and her companion are coming to visit. "What we need is a daybed," I said to Ed.

Our friend Sharon came to help paint. She said, "Could you use a daybed? My daughter was throwing hers out. I said, 'Don't do that, you paid a lot of money for it!' I stored it in my garage. If you want it, I'll bring it over." Exactly what we needed and we hadn't said a word! Last night, I reviewed the upcoming days in my head—painting; Mom, her helper, and Kentucky guests expected, plus ministry commitments. *I don't have sheets or anything for the daybed!* I'd have to squeeze shopping in somewhere.

Today, Sharon arrived with the beautiful bed. "I brought you a present," she said. She pulled mattress pads, sheets and pillows, shams and a bedspread from her van! God inspired Sharon to rescue the daybed when it was headed for the scrap pile. It arrived through the Holy Spirit's network. God moves people worldwide to meet needs. As more people are reborn into Christ's Body we'll see even greater things!

Every mission we've been on has examples of this worldwide Holy Spirit network in action. For instance, in 1997 a friend came from Kenya and prophesied, "Brazil is waiting for you." *Brazil, I thought, we don't know anyone in Brazil.* We kept Brazil in our minds and prayers. In 2006, we were on mission in Jamaica, West Indies. After a service, Brother Felipe, a Missionary of Mandeville, said, "God spoke two things to me. One, you should come to Brazil. Two, I should arrange translators, ministry, everything." In 2008 a team of four went to Brazil and the ministry was glorious. God healed many people—tumors disappeared, hearing was restored, and captives were set free.

Jesus may do greater things through His worldwide Body Ministry than when He led a small group of disciples in Israel who didn't have the Holy Spirit Baptism. When we work together under His headship in like-minded teams, we see more miracles because of His supernatural power flowing through more of us! Marvelous works occur worldwide because Christ speaks and His Body obeys with faith.

Bridge for Peace serves God and people in teams. Jesus chooses the teams and gives us complementary gifts. Some desire to serve in healing, others serve with administrative, technical, teaching, generous financial gifts, or prophetic word. Many have used their God-given talents to produce Bridge for Peace CDs, DVDs, this Workbook, other resources, and various anointed events.

4) Have you had experience with the Body Ministry? Please describe.

_____

_____

_____

_____

5) Can you describe an accomplishment achieved by Holy Spirit power through your participation in the Body Ministry that could not have succeeded otherwise?

_____

_____

_____

_____

It is amazing to realize Jesus Christ is alive in us and desires to use us for the healing ministry. I meet many people who believe in miracles, but find it is often difficult for them to believe:
    a) they can receive a miracle
    b) God will use them to heal others

The enemy of our soul will always try to stop us from moving into greater things. The Holy Spirit inspires us to the new and unusual. The Holy Spirit is creativity. We may tend to back away from a new and greater thing because it feels uncomfortable. Perhaps it has never been done before. Obedience may cost financially. We may have to step away from income producing situations or give more of our income to God's cause. We may have to humble ourselves to respond to the Holy Spirit's call, but obedience is rewarded.

A local man was driving when he heard the Lord say, "Pull over." He did. Then he heard the Lord say, "Kneel on top of your car." "What?" he wondered. "Kneel on top of your car," he heard the Lord say. Being familiar with God's voice in his heart, he had to decide. Would he obey or not? He climbed up and knelt on top of his car by the side of the road. Moments later, another car pulled behind him. The driver got out. He had tears in his eyes as he approached the kneeling man. Looking up to the man on the car roof he said, "I was just telling God, if You're real, let me see someone kneeling on top of their car praying to You, right here on this road.'"

Do you want to hear from the Lord and be used to bring people to Christ? Ask the Holy Spirit to reveal anything that is holding you back.

6) Discuss any personal obstacles to God's desire to use you for greater things.

_____

_____

_____

7) What might help you to move forward? Can you implement a plan to receive what you need?

_____

_____

_____

PERSEVERANCE vs. STRIVING

To fulfill our potential in Jesus Christ we have to persevere. James 1:4 says, "Perseverance must finish its work so that you may be mature and complete, not lacking anything."

Jesus released power at the cross for us to persevere. Those who call on His Name receive supernatural ability to persevere. We are God's vessels, the Holy Spirit works through us for God's glory. Apart from God we can do nothing.

When in Australia, we met Bishop Harry Westcott and stayed on his ranch. God has used him for many fantastic miracles. Some of the extraordinary healings God has performed through Bishop Harry have been recorded in Australian newspapers. God also uses Bishop Harry to train others in the gift of healing through Jesus Christ. One day, Bishop Harry was speaking at a church about the wondrous ways he'd been used by God. He testified to incredible miracles God had done through him. Suddenly he said, "*I can't heal a fly's eyeball!*" Bishop Harry does not strive. He knows miracles do not depend on him. At the same time, he knows how to persevere, continuing in prayer until the will of God has been made manifest.

James 5:16 says, "The earnest, heartfelt, and continued prayer of a righteous man makes tremendous power available, dynamic in its working." James describes perseverance as earnest, heartfelt, and continued prayer. Persevering prayer in the Name of Jesus and through His Blood makes unlimited, dynamic power available for the healing of the nations and the glory of God.

8) How would you describe perseverance?

_____

_____

_____

Elijah demonstrated that we become a vessel God can increasingly use through perseverance. James 5:17-18 says, "Elijah was as human as we are, and yet when he prayed earnestly that no rain would fall, none fell for the next three and a half years! Then he prayed for rain, and down it poured."

Scripture says Elijah was like us, he had a physical body, human emotions, and preferences like we do. The Word says simply that he prayed for it not to rain and then he prayed again and it rained. Let's take a closer look at this incident. (Read 1Kings 18:41-45.)

The simple recounting of Elijah's exploits in James expands into an exercise of faithful perseverance when we read scripture. James recounted Elijah's actions as a good example of perseverance. The book of Kings shows us Elijah's perseverance. Seven times he prayed and sent his servant. Seven times—again, again, again, again, again, again and again—Elijah prayed and sent his servant. Then the servant saw a small cloud rising from the sea. A small cloud was enough for Elijah to advise the king to hurry to avoid a rainstorm!

9) James tells us we can identify with Elijah. He was human, just like us. He was subject to feelings of enthusiasm, discouragement, elation, fear, hope, and despair. What kind of feelings have you experienced when persevering in prayer?

_____

_____

_____

_____

10) Can you give an example of perseverance from your life?

_____

There is a saying, "Pray like it depends on God, work like it depends on you." This motto encourages us in our efforts. While we labor hard, we do the work in obedience and know God supplies. Another favorite motto says, "We do the possible, God does the impossible." We are to step forward with the talents and resources God gives us, holding nothing back. Then we see God's miracles. We engage the work and persevere in it by faith. We may not see the possibilities of success in the natural realm. Yet, it is often when we near the threshold of the inability to move further, we see His supply. He tests us so that we know ourselves.

Jesus says, "Apart from me you can do nothing." (John 15:5b) Striving says, "It all depends on me." What is the root of striving? Some fear God won't come through, saying, "I'm afraid it depends on me." Manipulation, control, desire for attention, and pride distort perceptions. Some people in bondage to striving enjoy feeling that everything depends on them.

> **He tests us so that we know ourselves.**

Why do you go into "striving" mode? What is the underlying root? If we agree with deception, whatever it may be, we may strive to accomplish things for God in our own strength. If we believe "everything depends on me" we try to accomplish things for God from our own strength. If I fall into the trap of striving, whatever I undertake has to be possible for me to achieve, because I believe I'm the one who will do it. Striving is determination to make it happen without God's power, without desiring, seeking, or waiting on His Presence. When we are striving it is an effort from our own capacities, not a work of the Holy Spirit. We may find ourselves relying on methods rather than the Holy Spirit. Striving may end in bitterness, resentment, exhaustion, burn-out, joyless service, superiority, pride, or other undesirable outcomes.

11) Can you describe the difference between persevering and striving?

_____

_____

_____

12) To see the greater things, we have to be in obedience. What can help us discern whether a project is a God-idea or one of our good ideas?

_____

_____

_____

_____

13) Sometimes, we begin well and then get off the track by striving. Has this ever happened to you? What helps you notice you've taken ownership of what God began?

_____

_____

Barry served as mission photographer in Ghana. At times he joined us on the prayer team. On Barry's second Bridge for Peace mission he prayed for a man with a severe knee problem. After prayer, the man leapfrogged down the aisle. It was almost comical how he stood at the edge of the pews and kicked his foot out at the assembly to uproarious praise of the Lord. Barry later gave the testimony saying, "We prayed for quite awhile." I felt inspired to question him. "About how long was quite awhile?"
"About 15 to 20 minutes."
I asked the Ghanian people, "If you had an appointment at the doctor, would you have to wait 20 minutes?" The people explained they couldn't even get an appointment. They had to turn up and receive a ticket that would tell them when their appointment would be for that day. They could wait for hours. The speed of the healing was incredible. Yet, to Barry, it seemed he was praying "quite awhile".

14) Have you ever prayed for something that seemed to be taking "quite awhile"? How do you feel about it now and why?

_____

_____

_____

Read Mark 8:22-26. Jesus led the blind man out of the village. It seems Jesus not only took the blind man outside of his environment to an auspicious place, a more conducive place, but outside of his mentality as well. Jesus told the man, "Do not even go into the village," as if Jesus didn't want the newly healed man to associate with the villagers. Why didn't Jesus want him to go back there? Perhaps Jesus wanted the man to avoid skepticism.

Ed and I were at a party when a young lady told us she was discouraged over her diabetic condition that caused her eye and foot problems. We went into the bedroom where the guests' coats were stacked on the bed. As we prayed she said she was experiencing tingling in her foot. We kept praying. A guest entered to retrieve her coat. When she saw us praying, she backed out of the room and closed the door. Healing prayer is often surprising and unusual to people, but Jesus can use different settings to take us outside of our experience and lead us to a more spacious place of faith.

Jesus prayed and then asked a question. As one translation says, "Do you possibly see anything?" We take up the model and ask as Jesus did. When praying for others we ask them, "Do you see a change?" "Is there any difference?" "What is happening?"

The man experienced some change, Jesus prayed again. The Master prayed once, He prayed twice. The greater thing became manifest in the man's improved sight.

15) What do you think Jesus was saying to us by this example in Mark 8?

_____

_____

Read Jeremiah 12:3-5. Jeremiah views himself as devoted, but he is getting discouraged, impatient. He has been obedient, but he hasn't seen fruit. The Lord rebukes Jeremiah's impatience. God asks Jeremiah, "If you have raced with men on foot and they have tired you out, how can you compete with horses?"

Horses symbolize the might and power of the world. God wants us to embrace the small things, to begin at the beginning and progress to greater things. After all, only God can be the judge of the actual size of our obedience. Some people want to skip the trials that develop godly character and see the greater things. Jeremiah was discouraged because he didn't see the fruit he wanted. God was doing a greater work that Jeremiah couldn't see. God was developing fruit in Jeremiah; He was developing patience.

16) Can you remember a time when you identified with Jeremiah's feelings in this passage? Explain.

_____

_____

_____

17) Do you see a connection between perseverance and greater things in your life?

_____

_____

_____

God bless you today as we complete our time together. Thank you for taking up this course, I hope it has been a blessing. We'd like to hear how the course went for you. Please write us at bridgeforpeace@optonline.net with your input.

I pray we will grow in Holy Spirit wisdom and power and see the *greater things* God has planned for us. God will continue to urge us to live fully through His power and to glorify Him. God alone brings us fullness of joy. In all things, let us turn to Jesus, our Bridge for Peace.

Answer Key

Part One

ANSWER KEY

PART ONE
LESSON ONE

COVENANT

NOAH

1) Noah offered a burnt sacrifice, a blood sacrifice.

2) God promised to never again destroy the earth by flood.

ABRAHAM

3) Abraham offered a blood sacrifice of a heifer, goat, and ram.

4) God promised Abraham descendants beyond number who would endure 400 years of slavery, and then live in a land of their own from the Nile River in Egypt to the River Euphrates in Assyria.

5) Personal answer.

6) God asked that Abraham and his descendants be circumcised.

7) God's promises to Abraham:
    a) Abraham would be the Father of Nations.
    b) God would be their God.
    c) Abraham's descendants would live in a land of their own.

8) God asked Abraham to offer his son Isaac as a blood sacrifice.

9) Abraham built an altar, prepared wood to burn the sacrifice, tied Isaac, and placed him on the altar. Abraham took the knife to kill his son as a blood sacrifice.

10) God stopped Abraham from sacrificing Isaac and provided a ram for the sacrifice.

11) God said because Abraham was willing to sacrifice his only son, God would bless him with innumerable descendants who would defeat their enemies and be a blessing to the nations.

MOSES

12) If Moses would return to Egypt as God's messenger, God promised to rescue the Israelites from <u>slavery</u> and lead them to <u>a land flowing with milk and honey.</u>

13) God wanted the Israelites to obey Him.

14) God said the Israelites would be His own special treasure from among all nations. They would be as a kingdom of priests to Him. They would be His holy nation.

15) The Israelites said they would do everything God asked.

16) This is a paraphrase of the Ten Commandments found in Exodus 20 beginning with verse 3. Do not worship any other gods; v.4-6 do not make idols of any kind; v.7 do not misuse God's Name; v.8-11 keep the Sabbath holy; v.12 honor your parents; v.13 no murder; v.14 no adultery; v.15 no stealing; v.16 no lying; v.17 no coveting another's house, wife, servants, animals, or anything else they own.

17)   a) Moses recounted God's words.
       b) Moses wrote them down.
       c) Moses built an altar at the foot of the mountain.
       d) Moses sent young men to sacrifice bulls.
       e) Moses splashed half the animal blood against the altar.
        f) Moses read the Book of the Covenant to the Israelites.

18) The Israelites said they would obey God.

19) Moses sprinkled blood over the people.

20) Personal Answer.
A covenant is a binding and solemn agreement made by two or more individuals, or parties, to do or keep from doing a specific thing.

21) Moses said the blood confirmed the covenant the Lord made with them.

22) A mediator is a person in the middle, a go-between. A mediator may help two parties reach an agreement.

23) Personal Answer.
When I was a department head in a healthcare facility, union personnel could not reach an agreement with management.   A professional mediator was hired to establish a legal agreement.

ADAM AND EVE

24) Romans 3:23 says all have sinned and all fall short of God's glorious standard. We all sin. We disobey God, just like Adam and Eve.

25) Personal answer. Yes, I have sinned.

26) God said He would put His laws in our minds so we would understand them. He would write them in our hearts, and we would know the Lord. He said everyone will know God and God will forgive our wrongdoings and forget our sins (Hebrews 8:10-12).

27) Jesus Christ is the one mediator of the New Covenant.

28) Jesus Christ offered Himself in exchange for all sinners, to reconcile us to God and set us free from the death penalty due for our sin.

29) Jesus becomes an intimate companion through a love agreement. Jesus proposes I leave my old sinful life behind and enter into new permanent relationship and embrace new life with Him. Jesus made a public commitment at the cross, laying down His life for me. Jesus came to give me new life. He promises to love me and never leave me, as a groom promises his bride at their wedding. Jesus loves me completely. If I accept His proposal and commit myself to Jesus, I will live for Him on earth and be with Him in heaven for eternity.

30) Some Old and New Covenant differences are:

Old Covenant	New Covenant
Based on law	Based on love
Written in stone	Written on hearts
Mediator Moses	Mediator Jesus Christ
Taught by Moses	Taught by the Holy Spirit

31) Personal answer.

32) A covenant requires something of both parties. In the case of Jesus Christ crucified, the New Covenant, He gave His life for me.   To enter the New Covenant, I give my life to God. The covenant requires a noticeable, measurable impact on the recipient of the gift. I have received the gift of Christ crucified. A life change must be evident or I have not entered into covenant with God. If I do not make the exchange by giving my life to Jesus Christ to receive eternal life, a covenant does not exist.

33) Personal answer. I grow in my New Covenant relationship with God by spending time with Jesus Christ, talking, and sharing my heart with Him. When I read God's Word, my knowledge of God's New Covenant promises to me deepens and moves my heart.

ANSWER KEY

PART ONE
LESSON TWO

THE BLOOD COVENANT

ADAM and EVE

1) Adam and Eve made a covering of fig leaves.

2) God knew a man-made covering was inadequate and provided Adam and Eve a covering of animal skins (Genesis 3:21).

3) Animals had to die to provide animal skins.

ABRAHAM

4) God told Abraham to assemble a three-year old heifer, a three-year old goat, a three-year old ram, a turtledove, and a young pigeon.

5) Abraham cut the larger animals and laid their bodies side by side.

6) Personal answer. In 1989, I discerned God's invitation to allow Him to recreate my life. It would require ending my businesses. I did not renew my business licenses.

7) Personal answer. On the way home from a prayer meeting, a van rear-ended our Volvo crushing the car so severely it was declared "totaled." An ambulance brought Ed and me to the hospital. I remember looking at the tile ceiling, repeating God's promises as He put them into my mind. Once home, I remember reading God's healing promises again and again.

8) God caused Abraham to see a smoking fire pot pass through the cut animals.

9) Personal Answer. I meet God in nature, people, scriptural and prophetic revelations, dreams, visions, circumstances, miracles, provision, and physical sensations.

10) Personal answer. I remember the joy of April 6, 2008 when we celebrated groundbreaking for the home God had promised twenty years ago, in 1988.

11) God said Abraham's descendants would come through Isaac.

12) Personal answer.

I first heard this scripture as a little girl. I still remember the line drawing of Isaac on the altar. I felt confused. It didn't seem like a loving God would ask a man to sacrifice his son. Today I feel both grief at blood sacrifice and awesome wonder when I read this passage. I think of Abraham's incredible relationship with God and what this passage says about the Father and the Son's astonishing love for me—for us.

13) Personal answer comparing/contrasting your feelings about the sacrifice of Father Abraham with Father God's sacrifice.

I know God the Father loves perfectly. As much as Abraham loved Isaac, his love was only a shadow of the Father's capacity to love. Isaac was a faithful son, but his obedience was only a shadow of Jesus Christ's faithfulness. I know my feelings of being profoundly overwhelmed by Christ's sacrifice are shallow compared to the incomprehensible cost of God's sacrifice. I know the Father and Jesus Christ did it for me. I feel grateful and humbled. My feelings are mixed. At times, I hesitate to search out the depths of God's tremendous love, to feel it. I find it painful to be loved that completely because it mirrors back my lack of faithfulness. At the same time, I feel pure joy.

14) Isaac asked his father, "...where is the lamb for a burnt offering?"

15) Abraham tells Isaac God will provide Himself the lamb.

16) Abraham saw the coming of Jesus and was glad.

17) Personal answer. Yes, I can relate to Abraham's God-given vision. While suffering through the painful death of a friend, I've rejoiced knowing she is in heaven and we will be reunited because of Jesus Christ.

18) God's angel stopped Abraham from sacrificing Isaac.

19) God says because Abraham was willing to sacrifice his only son, God would bless him with innumerable descendants who would defeat their enemies and be a blessing to the nations.

20) Abraham sacrifices a ram he finds in a bush.

21) Jesus died for <u>sinners</u>. Jesus became our substitute. Jesus substituted his <u>life</u> for ours.

22) The penalty for sin is death.

23) We are freed from the death penalty through Jesus Christ our Lord.

24) Abraham says **they** will be back.

25) One possible meaning is that Abraham believed God could resurrect the dead.

26) Satan is the god of this world.

27) This world is under the power and control of satan.

28) Satan is the prince of the power of the air. He is at work in the hearts of the disobedient.

29) Satan would be thrown out as Jesus was crucified.

30) Personal answer. I've seen many people delivered from demonic power. I have also seen people blame satan rather than accept responsibility for their actions. Studying scripture has helped me to understand more about satan and the role of the believer in the world. I know we are to take dominion. We are not to be afraid, but we are to set the captives free in the Name of Jesus Christ and through His Blood.

MOSES

31) The two rooms were called the Holy Place and the Most Holy Place.

32) A curtain separated the Holy Place from the Most Holy Place.

33) The Holy Place had a lamp stand and a table with loaves of holy bread on it.

34) The Most Holy Place or the Holy of Holies had a gold incense altar and the Ark of the Covenant, or the Ark of Testimony.

35) The Ark of the Covenant contained a gold jar filled with manna, Aaron's staff, and the Ten Commandments. For more details about manna read Exodus 16:4-17. For more details about Aaron's staff read Numbers17:1-10.

36) God would meet with Moses at set times, talk with him, and give His commands for Israel from above the atonement cover between the angels.

37) Personal answer. It must have been discouraging, even leading to self-disgust and hopelessness. If sin was committed an hour after the animal substituted for a person, the whole process would begin again.

38) This system couldn't get to the heart of the matter, it couldn't cleanse consciences.

39) The high priest could enter only with blood.

40) The blood's purpose was to cover the sin of the high priest and the people.

41) God could only be approached with <u>blood</u>.

JESUS CHRIST

42) Through His shed blood Jesus has forgiven our sins, rescued us from satan, restored us to God's Kingdom, and purchased our freedom.

43) Jesus Christ is eternal High Priest.

44) Jesus Christ has entered the heavenly sanctuary.

45) When Jesus Christ was crucified the temple curtain was torn from top to bottom.

46) Each year a high priest would be chosen to enter the Holy of Holies taking with him the blood of an animal, the only way to approach God. Jesus Christ entered the heavenly Holy of Holies not by the blood of animals but by His own Blood. He established a new system, the New Covenant, by becoming the perfect sacrifice for the atonement of sin, becoming our substitute. In the Old Covenant, only the high priest could enter. In the New Covenant we can approach God through the perfect blood sacrifice made for us by Jesus Christ.

47) We can approach God only through the Blood of Jesus Christ.

48) Blood was required as proof of death.

49) Only by Jesus Christ's death, Blood, and substitution do we receive our inheritance.

50) Personal answer. I pray the Blood of Jesus for people because New Covenant life, authority, healing, deliverance, miracle working power, provision, and more are in the Blood of Jesus.

ANSWER KEY

PART ONE
LESSON THREE

INHERITANCE

1) Personal answer. Yes, I want to understand more about the inheritance Jesus secured for me. I know my inheritance is salvation, healing, deliverance, and provision.

2) Personal answer. Yes. I know I am named in a will.

3) Death has to be established for a will to take effect. A will is in effect after a man dies. A will has no power at all while the man who created it lives.

4) Personal answer. Resurrection of the dead refers to life in the glorified body Christ has already prepared for me after my physical death. Through Adam I inherited death. Jesus Christ became my substitute and through Him I have been made alive both while in the flesh and after physical death.

5) God so loved the world that He gave His only Son so that everyone who believes in Him will not perish but will receive eternal life. God did not send his Son into the world to condemn it, but to save it (John 3:16-17).

6) Personal choice of translation substituting your name. (For example: God so loved Annette that He gave His only Son...)

7) Personal story of sozo power at work. As an example, I shared the experience of God's power manifested for me at the airport and on the plane.

8) Personal answer. My life demonstrates my inheritance as I know I have received salvation from Him. My testimony includes personal miraculous healings and deliverances as well as incredible stories of a myriad of needs met by the Lord for His glory.

9) Personal Answer. Yes, I'm confident through my experience of God's faithfulness and His demonstration of the power of His Word and the gift of faith.
For further study on inheritance read 1Peter chapter 1.

10) Personal answer. As life continually changes, I am increasingly grateful for unfolding of the inheritance I have received. As life becomes more demanding and I lean more on the Lord, I find I know more of the solid strength of My Rock.

Bridge for Peace Foundation for Healing

11) Personal answer. I am confident that Jesus Christ has ensured my salvation and I thank God for the gift.

12) Personal answer. For me the Holy Spirit works in scripture, the anchor image, the experience of anchors while boating, the image of the curtain as a veil between heaven and earth to help me visualize and express Jesus as my anchor behind the veil.

13) Personal testimony. Not all dying people we pray for go to the Lord immediately as in these examples. However, we persevere for their peaceful passing to the Lord. One man we prayed for refused to accept the Lord's covenant invitation for several months. Thank God, he received Jesus before he died.

HEALING
14) Personal healing testimony of what you experienced or the experience of someone you know or read about.

DELIVERANCE
15) Personal deliverance testimony of you or someone you know experiencing freedom through God's intervention.

PROVISION
16) Personal provision testimony. Witness to how God met a need.

17) Personal answer. I find Isaiah 53 appropriate for every circumstance. During the laying on of hands or over the phone I pray, "You took all of our infirmities and You healed all of our diseases. By your stripes, Lord, we are healed."

ANSWER KEY

PART ONE
LESSON FOUR

WHY DID JESUS DIE FOR US?

1) Personal answer.
I am amazed when I notice what seems to be a sudden burst of new freedom, joy, peace, or awareness of God's abundance. The Holy Spirit continually works in my life taking me to new levels of felt grace.

2) Personal answer.
I've had the experience of being torn between choices. I remember specific occasions when grace overcame all resistance instantaneously because I recalled Galatians 2:20. I often quote this scripture out loud, sometimes in an empty room! To live out of Galatians 2:20, knowing I have been crucified with Christ, gives me a feeling of serenity and a sense of victory.

3) Personal answer.
Yes. Sometimes it seems the pressure to conform increases as people try to make sense of a crazy world. Some must feel the way out of darkness is by establishing stricter rules. I find myself increasingly aware of external expectations as God strips me of false teachings. Paul was keenly aware of man-made rules that either opposed or were man-made additions to God's requirements. I'm blessed to have a few people like Paul in my life who have helped me grow in discernment.

4) Personal answer.
Trying to keep external rules focuses me on two things: what other people think and measuring my success. I know God isn't interested in either. God wants my focus to be on what He thinks as explained in His Word and to measure my success by my obedience to His Word. God does give me power to keep His rules. God says He has written His law on my heart. Of course, mankind interprets God's rules and that becomes the impetus for personal study and prayer for discernment as life situations arise.

5) Personal answer.
Trying to overcome my own sin leads to frustration, makes the sin really large in my life, and has never been successful. Bringing my sin to the Lord and struggling with my own darkness to embrace His ways have thankfully yielded revelation and peace. When struggling with sin, I apply God's remedy of repentance, receiving forgiveness, relying on His overcoming grace, and submission to the Holy Spirit Who continues to change my life.

6) Personal answer.

God's law on my heart is the still small voice. His Word says I'll always hear a voice behind me saying, "This is the way, walk in it." God's Word is often confrontational and I know the difference between my inner challenge to respond to Him and my striving to meet expectations set up by others through a set of rules—spoken or unspoken. God's requirements lead to life. Ungodly rules are like sneak thieves, robbing us a little at a time, eventually leading to spiritual poverty and death.

7) Personal answer.

My testimony on the Bridge for Peace CD "Hold onto the Vision" details how God led me to take risks. I am so very grateful for how God has recreated my life.

8) Personal answer.

I'm still submitting. He's still growing me! Most recently, I've been writing this course as a response to the Holy Spirit. God has been growing me through the writing. Another place of growth has been the privilege of working with gifted Bridge for Peace folks who freely shared their expertise and encouragement to complete this work! God moved in a new way as we collaborated to put this course together. Though I often work with mission teams, while completing this assignment, I've experienced a new dimension of unity under Christ's headship. God breathed a rich fragrance into the Bridge for Peace publishing team, pilot study groups, and every aspect of preparing this book for print. God birthed the anointing through submission and collaboration. I highly value the experience.

9) Personal answer.

I still find I sometimes resist meeting Him in the depths to which He invites me. Meeting God is a formidable event! It's always glorious, but often scary to go there.

10) Personal answer.

God's call on my life and to Bridge for Peace is healing to the nations. Through His grace I continue to respond to His leading. Healing is a broad ministry. God's carefully trained me and the Holy Spirit continues to show me new areas He wants to address through me. Most recently, God is directing me to pray for suicidal people or those impacted by suicide. Jesus wants to set them free through His Blood.

11) Personal name substitution.

Annette has been crucified with Christ. It is no longer Annette who lives, but Christ (The Messiah) lives in Annette; and the life Annette lives in the body, she lives by faith in the Son of God Who loves her and gave Himself for her.

<u>Answer Key</u>

<u>Part Two</u>

ANSWER KEY

PART TWO
LESSON ONE

AUTHORITY I

1) Personal answer.
Jesus Christ was born on earth as a man. He purposefully humbled Himself and determined to obey the Father without limitation, willing even to die on a cross, a despicable death to the people of His time. Though many reviled Him, God exalted Jesus to the highest place. The Father gave Jesus a name above every name. There is a heavenly decree demanding that at the Name of Jesus every knee shall bow, and every tongue confess that Jesus Christ is Lord. "Every" includes spiritual and physical beings.

2) Personal answer.
Scripture says the Name of Jesus is above every name. To me that means Jesus Christ is the highest authority.

3) Personal answer.
An ambassador officially represents the government of one country to the government of another. An ambassador usually lives in a foreign land during assignment. Christ's followers represent the Kingdom of Heaven with God's full authority to earth and demonic forces. As an ambassador of Christ, I represent His Kingdom on earth. I consider myself a foreigner on assignment in this world, personally preferring heaven, but serving wholeheartedly for the sake of the One Who saved me. He wants none to perish in hell, but all to come to know Him. My responsibility is to obey His will on a daily basis. My assignment includes proclaiming the good news that His Kingdom has come, healing the sick, delivering the demonized.

4) Personal answer.
Once, in an airport elevator, I had occasion to speak to a man who did not know Jesus Christ. I told him some of my experiences. When I was sharing about a blind person he said, "Don't tell me he was healed." He refused to hear. As the elevator doors opened he said, "All I need is God to give me a million dollars." As I was leaving the elevator a Jamaican flight attendant looked at him and said, "All you need is to know Jesus Christ is Lord." I was so delighted to meet another ambassador for Christ! I pray the man heard the message.

5) Jesus says all authority in heaven and earth has been given to Him. He commands his disciples, those under Him, to train, baptize, instruct, and commission others. Jesus gives His followers authority.

6) Jesus gave his followers supernatural grace, physical and mental strength, and ability to overcome the power the enemy possesses. Spirits would have to submit to His followers because of God's authority. Jesus gives authority over sickness to His believers. He says His ambassadors will speak the language of His Kingdom through the gift of tongues. Jesus says nothing shall in any way harm them. That's diplomatic immunity!

7) Jesus said He would drive out demons and heal people today and tomorrow. Today, tomorrow, and on the third day He knew He had authority and would continue His work.

8) Personal answer.
There may be various ways we receive God's assurance, but there is only one way we can be effective. All success comes from God. His obedient servants will be effective and give Him all the glory.

9) Personal answer.
God assures me daily through prayer as I read His Word. I am so grateful for the assurance He has produced in me, but I expect to continue to grow in God-assurance!

10) Personal answer.
As the Holy Spirit leads me to study and pray the Word, listen to Christian CDs, read books, attend conferences, and go out on mission, I grow in God assurance. Obeying His Word to lay hands on the sick, doing His Word, releases great growth spurts!

11) His disciples said demons obeyed them when they used authority given in the Name of Jesus.

12) Personal Answer.
When I first began in deliverance ministry at times it seemed surreal. I remember thinking at times, "What is happening here?" The Holy Spirit has led me through many experiences with the demonic. My Teacher is awesome! Now my feeling about deliverance ministry is deep gratitude to Jesus Christ who set us free by His cross and continues to minister freedom through His disciples.

13) Personal example.
I prayed for a woman with trigeminal neuralgia, called suicide disease. It is extremely painful, with no known cure or treatment. Victims of the disease often despair. Through the authority of the Name of Jesus, the lady was healed. Glory to our God Whose authority is ultimate!

ANSWER KEY

PART TWO
LESSON TWO

AUTHORITY II

IMPORTANCE OF A NAME

1) Personal Answer.
Names reflect character and purpose. I think God renamed people to express to them who they had become and/or who they would become. Given names also expressed potential and destiny.

2) Personal Answer.
Annette means grace, graceful, little Anne. It reflects my French background. My mother's father was raised in France.

3) Personal Answer.
My name is very significant to me. By grace I was saved! There are several scriptures concerning "grace" that bless me because my name means grace. I embrace my implied destiny of being grace-full!

4) Personal Answer.
I am always eager to hear what God will speak through His Body when two or more are present. I have experienced Holy Spirit teachings, prophetic words and song, and inspired praise when praying with others. His Presence expressed in the body is a source of strength, encouragement, direction, and joy.

PRAYING IN THE NAME OF JESUS

5) Personal choice and discussion.
"Ask" is repeated three times. God wants us to ask. "In My Name" is also repeated three times. "I will do it" is repeated twice. I note two other phrases in these scriptures:
      1) "He will grant your request."
      2) "He will give it to you."
I find the repetition of these themes faith-building.

6) Personal answer.
Jesus taught the "Our Father" showing He desires us to pray "Your will be done." At one time I thought it was a prayer of resignation. I know now it is a prayer of acceptance and determination.

ABUSE OF POWER

7) Personal answer.
History abounds with power struggles and they still surround us in many different forms. I see goodness in God's power. In the healing ministry I see people set free through God's power. I have seen people crippled by abusive power as sickness passes from parents to children. Tragically, children may continue the pattern of abuse in their own families. When I hear stories of power abuse I feel conflicting emotions of anger, sadness, and hope for the healing of victims. I feel power issues cannot be ignored.

8) Personal answer.
At first it was hard for me to speak in the Name of Jesus. I hadn't understood the authority God had entrusted to me or the response required of me. I had been taught about my unworthiness. The Holy Spirit showed me these teachings were more about false humility than God's Word and plan. I am grateful to the Holy Spirit who continues to teach truth about God's power. I thank God for giving me the gift of the Name of His Son Jesus Christ.

9) Personal answer.
Bertha, an elderly friend in a wheelchair, sent money to a televangelist because he said it would affect her healing.

10) Personal Answer.
As we wait on the Holy Spirit, I find He brings memories or reveals current situations that require forgiveness. Unforgiveness damages people. Though an abuser may not have asked for forgiveness, God asks me to choose forgiveness and then pours healing into a soft heart. The Holy Spirit waits for our permission to set us free.

11) Personal answer.
As an American, I often take for granted the power I have to influence. My choice of how I spend money is power. The ability I have to vote, to write letters of protest, to speak life-giving words, are all issues concerning how I use my power. When I negate or don't exert my power appropriately, I have to repent.

IDENTITY THEFT

12) Personal answer.
I have to stand my ground and remind myself of scriptural truths. Robbery attempts are the norm in this world, but the Name of the Lord is a strong tower (Proverbs 18:10)! I liberally call on Jesus' Name. I defend myself from satan's lies with the Word and I use scripture as an offensive weapon against the enemy driving him back. Remember, robberies are the norm and, as Christians, we are at high risk for an attack. My identity in Christ grows as the Holy Spirit teaches me through the Word, books, Bible studies, tapes, and experiences.

RIGHTEOUSNESS

13) Personal answer.
A self-righteous person believes he/she is good and approves of himself/herself on basis of personal goodness. A self-righteous person approves of himself or herself as good and bases that approval on contributions. The Bible cautions us, reminding us every man is right in his own eyes. The self-righteous are prone to measuring and striving. The result is usually either sinful pride or discouragement from performance failures. Jesus said only God is good. The righteous person has entered into the Blood Covenant, been washed by the Blood, and restored to God's inheritance. The righteous person has the authority of the Name of Jesus. The righteous person is in right-standing with God.

14) Personal answer.
Intercessory prayer releases God's power into circumstances. All people in authority need prayer. Government officials, religious leaders, teachers, parents, financial and industrial heads, and workers all need prayer to use their authority in godly ways. Children in school need prayer; babies in the womb need prayer. Jesus calls us to release power through intercession that His Father may be glorified.

ANSWER KEY

PART TWO
LESSON THREE

HOLY SPIRIT EMPOWERMENT

PASSOVER

1) Personal answer.
Some of their reactions were noticeable because Jesus mentioned they looked sad or filled with grief. Grief takes strange forms. Feelings of devastation, denial, numbness, pain, abandonment, and others are associated with grief. I remember how I have felt when people I loved drew closer to their death. Recalling those experiences, I imagine how the disciples may have felt and reacted.

2) Jesus said it was better for the disciples if He went because the Counselor, Friend, Comforter, Advocate would come.

THE HOLY SPIRIT

3) Jesus says the Spirit will guide them into truth they are not yet ready to receive. The Advocate will convict them of sin, explain righteousness and judgment. The Spirit will tell them what has been heard in heaven. The Friend will tell them about the future. The Comforter will bring revelation, telling the disciples what Jesus is saying. The Counselor will teach them and glorify Jesus.

4) Personal answer.
I treasure the Holy Spirit for all of these functions in my life. Particularly at this moment I feel especially grateful for conviction of sin. The Holy Spirit is the only One who can convict me, give me the grace to repent, and receive forgiveness through Jesus Christ.

5) Personal Answer.
I love and exalt the Holy Spirit. I am so grateful for His tender Presence. The Holy Spirit is the finest Teacher with perfect timing, knowing when I'm ready for the next lesson. He carefully prepares me and provides opportunity to apply His teaching so it becomes a part of me. The Holy Spirit is my Friend and I'm grateful to be His. Jesus described the Spirit as very important, and I've found that to be true.

6) Personal Answer.
Several occasions were important in my continual quest to know the Holy Spirit. I still remember the teaching on the Holy Spirit that was central to my confirmation experience. That's the earliest introduction I remember. Years later, as an adult, I attended a Life in the Spirit Seminar that also focused on the Holy Spirit. At the near conclusion of the seminar, I was blessed to receive the life-changing experience of the Presence and gifts of the Holy Spirit.

7) Some translations say when the disciples saw Him they worshipped, but doubted. Other versions say they all worshipped our resurrected Jesus, but *some* doubted. Several of them did not seem to have much faith.

8) They were to wait for the Baptism of the Holy Spirit.

9) Jesus said they'd receive power and would tell people about Him to the ends of the earth.

10) Personal answer.
I believe Jesus considered the Baptism of the Holy Spirit vital for every believer to complete his or her godly purpose. Jesus reemphasizes the importance of the Baptism of the Holy Spirit in several scripture passages.

PENTECOST

11) Personal answer.
I was invited to a charismatic prayer group and heard people speaking in tongues and sharing scripture passages with understanding. I loved Jesus, but saw that these people had something I didn't have. They said it was the Holy Spirit. I wanted the Holy Spirit. Throughout the seminar they explained scriptures relating to the Holy Spirit Baptism. They prayed for me and I received the Baptism of the Holy Spirit. I was wary of the gift of tongues, but received some very good advice. A prayer group leader said if anyone wanted the Holy Spirit Baptism, receive whatever the Holy Spirit had to give with gratitude. I'm glad I followed his advice.

12) Personal Answer.
Yes, when attending a Life in the Spirit Seminar. Ed received the Baptism of the Spirit in our living room.

13) Personal Answer. If you want to receive the Baptism of the Holy Spirit, pray the prayer in the next lesson! If someone you know wants to receive Holy Spirit Baptism, the prayer in the next lesson may help.

ANSWER KEY

PART TWO
LESSON FOUR

BLOOD COVENANT PRAYER

POWER FOR HEALING

1) Personal answer. God has shown me it is very important to give people an opportunity to receive the Holy Spirit. Sometimes the devil has tempted me to look at a person or a couple and think, "*They're* not interested." The devil lies. I don't want to go to bed after a healing service and wonder what God would have done if I had invited someone to receive the Holy Spirit. Looking back, I can't remember one person who came to me at a service for healing prayer who did *not* want to receive the Baptism of the Holy Spirit.

2) Personal answer. I believe it is very important to invite people to receive the Baptism of the Holy Spirit. I believe it is by power of the Holy Spirit that we are able to obediently live the life God intended for us. It is my responsibility to offer that equipping to people who are seeking help from the Lord.

POWER FOR EQUIPPING

3) Personal answer. I need the Holy Spirit to show me where to spend my energy and right now to equip me to be a sensitive servant to complete this Course as God intended.

POWER FOR REPENTANCE

4) Personal Answer. Yes. After a misunderstanding, I apologized for my part in the situation, and asked forgiveness from the person and from God. I had an incredible sense of God's presence after repentance. Joy and peace overflowed my spirit.

5) Personal Answer. My parents were married for over forty years. They had good relationships with their siblings and kept in frequent contact with other family members. There were arguments, but they were resolved.

6) Personal Answer. I know several people who have been wronged, but the abusive party refuses to own their responsibility. I have compassion for people in that situation.

7) Personal answer. Yes. Some of my thoughts and actions that I found acceptable ten years ago, I don't find acceptable today. I attribute this to God speaking to me about repentance.

POWER FOR FORGIVENESS

8) Personal Answer.
I need to forgive others; and sometimes I need to forgive myself. At times, when I thought I had forgiven, I later discover more forgiveness is needed. God wants me to choose forgiveness and the Holy Spirit helps me.

9) Personal answer.
I have found power through the Holy Spirit to make the decision to forgive.

10) Personal answer.
Jesus told us to love our enemies, to pray for them. Jesus demonstrated forgiveness of His enemies. Jesus did not, and does not, condone evil.

Answer Key

Part Three

ANSWER KEY

PART THREE
LESSON ONE

FOUR MANIFESTATIONS OF HEALING

1) Personal answer.
In relation to physical healing, whenever the physical body recovers from illness it is a miracle.

2) Personal answer.
Paul spoke about bringing the gospel to the people with a demonstration of power. He didn't bring the gospel in his own strength. People embraced the truth by supernatural means and that demonstrated God's power. Jesus preached good news with the laying on of hands, miraculously healing the sick. Paul preached the gospel as his Master taught. Paul healed the sick in the Name of Jesus Christ, demonstrating God's power to glorify the Father.

3) Personal answer.
I have seen the gospel preached with the demonstration of power in Bridge for Peace when people received the truth that Jesus Christ is Lord. I have seen many realize God's word is true as God demonstrated His miraculous power, healing people and delivering them from demonic oppression while the being proclaimed.

4) Personal answer.   People always seem to be the most affected when I am simply myself and share my story. I guess that's why God sent me to those particular people in the first place, because He knows that I (my personality, experience, mannerisms) would be the most effective way to reach them. God knows which ambassador to send to each territory!

5) Personal answer.
It's difficult to enter into people's pain with them, but I have always found it a privilege.

6) Personal answer.
People need encouragement to persevere, to continue to go to healing services, to pray for themselves, to ask for intercession from their churches and friends. We help people when we encourage them to pursue every opportunity God gives them to receive their inheritance.

7) Personal answer.
When I was small all of my teeth fell out and were replaced with a full set—only larger! How amazing!

8) Personal answer.
Yes. Recently we prayed for a family member with thrush. It was amazing to see scabs form so quickly on the lips and inflammation of the tongue normalize. Then the scabs disappeared in an amazingly short period of time.

9) Personal answer.
Yes. A dear friend was diagnosed with scleroderma. As time passes her condition is improving instead of the expected worsening. At her last visit the doctor, who specializes in her condition, said, "You are way ahead of everyone else who is coming to see me." She attributes this to prayer.

10) Personal answer.
I think it is very important to share healing testimonies while praying for people. When we share stories of healing, we release faith. Everyone needs to be encouraged. I have heard many testimonies about people who woke up healed the day after the service. I pass on the story to encourage people to believe for their own healing. Also, many who have been healed before my eyes still hesitate to believe it.

Recently a man with a high-level position in the United Nations came for prayer. Communication was fundamental to his career. He underwent surgery for a heart condition and experienced a stroke on the operating table. As a result, he had aphasia; his speech was minimal and senseless. Both he and his wife were deeply grieved by his inability to work. After we prayed for him, he told us what happened to him. He was working in South Africa when this calamity hit. He expressed himself very well, with order and clarity. Then he said, "One day I'll be healed." One day! He was healed then. Even his wife said, "When we came here, you couldn't speak more than three words." The gentleman needed to be encouraged to own what Jesus Christ had done for him and made manifest that night at the service.

11) Personal answer.
Yes. Two days ago a man told me this story. I'd prayed for him last year for healing of a blood clot. After heart surgery a blood clot had formed on his heart. After prayer, he returned to the doctor for scheduled testing. Looking at the evidence, the doctor said, "I don't understand this. I can't find the blood clot. This is most unusual..."

12) Personal answer.
I am excited by Jesus Christ's straightforward words and direct promises to me. God's words cause me to examine my life for the expected fruit. There is comfort in Christ's Words. When people (sometimes churchgoers) are skeptical, cynical or condescending when you share about miraculous healings, remember Christ commanded us to deliver and heal, no matter what others think. I find it reassuring to know if I continue to do what God calls me to, He will fulfill His promises to me and glorify His Name in the process.

13) Personal answer.
Yes. Most recently I prayed for a woman who had panic attacks. I put my hand on her shoulder and had barely spoken a word when she instantaneously slumped in the pew. I wondered to myself if it was real or if she was acting. I met her two weeks later and she hadn't had a single attack.

ANSWER KEY

PART THREE
LESSON TWO

QUALIFIED TO MINISTER

1) Personal Answer.
I believe every person who is living the exchanged life is qualified to minister healing in their God-given sphere of influence. It would help me if the person listened to my request, demonstrated respect for me, and if I saw healings manifested when they prayed for others. To know they were a part of a praying group of people I respected would also be a help.

2) Personal Answer.
I am discerning when receiving ministry. I like to hear Holy Spirit approval regarding people I don't know. If someone I don't know is exceptionally eager to lay hands on me, I am most cautious. I am grateful to be surrounded by people who are living the exchanged life and willing to pray for me. I am also eager for prayer from people God has used as prophets in my life and seek it out whenever possible.

3) Personal Answer.
In the 1970s I received minimal encouragement. In the group I attended, there were definitely people who were considered by the leadership to be "qualified" to minister. (Actually, it was the leadership! They considered themselves qualified.) I was close to the leaders, and so participated on occasion. I also prayed for some people as the need arose outside of our meeting. However, in the 1980s God sent Ed and me to people who empowered us and were instrumental in our continued training. In 2000, when we cried out to God to see more of His healing power released, He sent us others to teach us, further our understanding, and encourage us.

4) Personal Answer.
God has done so much for me as I've ministered in healing. He has changed my mindset as I've studied His word. The blind see, the lame walk, the deaf hear, and I'm a part of that. And *still* I hear Him whisper of greater things. I want to see the healing of some conditions I haven't seen yet. I believe He is increasing my faith and trust, training me in instant obedience, and preparing me for greater things through the testings of the healing ministry.

5) Personal Answer.
I still want to see congenital diseases healed instantaneously. I've read about it and I believe He will allow me to see cystic fibrosis, muscular dystrophy, cerebral palsy, sickle-cell anemia, and other diseases healed.

6) Personal Answer.
Yes. However, I've found God's word is true and His promise will come to pass, if I believe and obey Him.

7) Personal Answer.
I am always seeking out people I can learn from. Whether traveling with Bridge for Peace in team, prayer group, or assisting in another ministry, I find submission to the voice of the Spirit key to my growth. One of the greatest thrills is hearing the confirmed Word of God through the Body. I have observed a few people who have resisted submitting to spiritual authority and they are not in a. blessed position at this time. Of course we are discussing *godly* spiritual authority

8) Personal Answer.
Companioning a sick person in prayer raises strong feelings. It can be emotionally and physically wearing, but is a precious experience and I have been grateful to God for it. Ultimately, my relationship with God has deepened from experiences with sick or dying people. It is very important to attend to self-care in intense times of companioning someone else. With the reality of time limitations, it may seem impossible. I firmly believe God shows me how to best spend time. I know I am dear to Him and He will lead me to invest time, even a few minutes, to revitalize myself. He desires my obedience in taking care of myself. Some-times, when we see desperate situations, we can forget we have needs as well as the sick person. It is important to listen to the Spirit in all things.

9) Personal Answer It
Yes. I remember seeking healing prayer for a physical situation. The healing minister asked me strange questions. Then she told me that she had various impressions that did not resonate with me at all. I felt angry. As a result, I decided I needed to forgive and prayed *for the person to be used by God.*
On two occasions I remember the healing minister tried to push me down to imitate what is sometimes called resting in the Spirit. Resting in the Spirit sometimes happens when people receive prayer. Resting in the Spirit is a genuine and spontaneous move of God, not a shove from the healing minister. Forgiveness was in order again and prayer.

10) Personal Answer.
The healing ministry is simple and complicated at the same time! God who called me will continue to qualify me.

ANSWER KEY

PART THREE
LESSON THREE

WHEN YOU DON'T SEE HEALING

1) Personal answer.
I have prayed for the healing of someone who subsequently died. A friend, a believer from another state, telephoned me. She said her Aunt Mary, who was a kind and loving person, was very sick with cancer. My friend felt bad about being so far away from her and asked if I could pray with her aunt. She had received miraculous healing from cancer some fifteen years prior. At that time, she was seriously ill in the hospital, when a great light entered her room and she knew she was healed. The doctors verified her unexplained healing.

When I met Mary, the colon cancer was advanced. She refused treatment and believed the Lord would heal her. When we prayed for her at our prayer meeting the Lord led me to a scripture. I didn't look for it or make it up. God presented it to me and I was amazed. It has been many years, but I recall it as saying Mary would live in the land of the living. (There are scriptures on that line in Psalms.) I wondered what it meant, because earth is the land of the living and heaven is the land of the living. I hesitated to read it to her, but I did.

Mary came for prayer at our prayer group a few times and we spoke on the phone a few times. She became sicker and died. We went to her wake. I felt sad about Mary dying, but grateful to know she was with Christ. I wondered how her family would feel about our coming to the wake, since we had prayed for Mary. Her husband expressed gratitude to me for our prayers and support. I was told Mary's grandniece addressed the mourners, telling them Mary was not dead but alive. She appealed for all in attendance to realize there is eternal life and it will be spent in heaven, the land of the living, or hell, the place of death.

2) Personal answer.
I felt sad and confused.

3) Personal answer.
I still don't understand why Mary wasn't healed, but I know she is rejoicing in eternity. Even though I don't have an answer, I don't feel so confused. Mary's death and life in the land of the living are both mysteries. I feel at peace. I trust the Lord will reveal what He desires to me about Mary's death and I wait upon Him with patience. I found less talk and more prayer helped.

4) Personal answer.
I still ask the Lord many questions and seek scriptural answers. Ed and I discuss the wonderful healings we see the Lord perform and also counsel with each other. Being able to share with the Bridge for Peace team on mission is the best situation because we are all together after the ministry. Local ministry is more difficult since we all go to our own homes afterward and it may be a few days before a situation can be discussed.

5) Personal Answer.
To help someone forgive, I would listen closely to the Holy Spirit. I might encourage them by telling them forgiveness is a choice not a feeling and they are the only one who can make the choice. I might tell them how unforgiveness hurts them and speak about how Jesus forgives us. I might share a story similar to theirs. I might talk with them about how forgiveness sets them free. The Holy Spirit knows the key to each heart. I would do all I could to be His instrument of deliverance from unforgiveness.

6) Jesus shouted to dead Lazarus to come out of the tomb and Lazarus walked out.

7) Personal observation.
When I read the scripture I note that Lazarus' resurrection did not depend on his faith. He was dead.

8) Personal observation.
Martha lamented Lazarus' death and believed her brother would not have died if Jesus had been there. She said even then she knew whatever Jesus asked from God would be granted. Jesus told her Lazarus would rise again. Martha affirmed it in the future sense. She didn't express any belief in her brother being raised back to earthly life. Mary also said she believed Jesus could have healed Lazarus. Some of the crowd blamed Jesus for not preventing Lazarus' death. None expressed faith that Lazarus could be resurrected. They resisted rolling away the stone from his tomb.

9) Personal observation.
Jesus acted on faith.

10) Personal observation.
When Jesus visited His home town He spoke wisdom and performed miracles.

11) Personal observation.
The people of Nazareth said He was a carpenter whose family they knew.

12) Personal observation.
They disapproved of Him and did not acknowledge His authority. They lacked faith in Him.

13) Jesus said, "A prophet is not without honor except in his country and among relatives and in his house."

14) Personal observation.
Jesus marveled because of their unbelief.

15) Personal observation.
Because of the Nazarenes' unbelief, Jesus couldn't do any mighty miracles among them except place hands on a few sick people and heal them. Their lack of faith hindered the miracles.

16) Personal observation.
Jairus was a local synagogue leader, the father of a very sick girl.

17) Personal observation.
Jairus asked Jesus to come to his home, lay hands on his daughter, and heal her. He had faith. He believed Jesus could heal.

18) The messenger said not to bother Jesus because Jairus' daughter was dead. The NLT translation says, "There's no use." They had no hope.

19) Personal observation.
He ignored them.

20) Personal answer.
I feel I get to know Him better through His response.

21) Personal observation.
Jesus asked Jairus
    a) not to be afraid
    b) to trust Him

22) Personal observation.
The crowd laughed at Jesus. I notice their laughter didn't seem to affect His plan.

23) Personal observation.
Jesus stopped the crowd from following and allowed only Peter, James, and John to go with him and Jairus. Mourners were inside the house. Jesus told them to go outside. He allowed only the girl's mother and father and His three disciples to be present when He told the little girl to "Get up." Perhaps, He only wanted people with faith or hope to be there.

24) Personal answer.
Jairus didn't discourage Jesus from coming to his home even though the messengers said his daughter was dead. Jairus didn't laugh when Jesus said the girl was asleep. Jairus knew as a synagogue leader that a dead body was unclean. He knew Jesus was breaking rules. Yet, Jairus obediently followed Jesus' instructions. His wife did not protest, but obeyed. They must have had faith in Jesus to obey these unusual instructions and allow Him to take charge in their home.

25) The daughter's miracle did not depend on her faith. She was dead.

26) Personal answer.
Jesus demonstrated faith even when the messenger, the crowd who saw the miracles, and the crowd of mocking mourners in the house did not. Jairus, his wife, Peter, James, and John did not express belief, but Jesus allowed their presence. Jesus knew who He wanted present—possibly those He knew had faith, could have faith or at least hope. He didn't want mockers or gawkers there. I noticed Jesus found it important to create a certain atmosphere by only permitting specific people to be present.

27) Personal observation.
The disciples tried to cast out an evil spirit, but could not.

28) Personal observation.
Jesus declared them to be stubborn, faithless people. Jesus asked, "How long must I be with you until you believe? How long must I put up with you?" Jesus said they didn't have enough faith to cast out the demon.

29) Personal observation.
The examples seem contrary as they pertain to faith. In John 11, it seems only the faith of Jesus the Healer mattered. The miracle took place despite what anyone else believed. In Mark 6, Jesus Himself was limited by other people's unbelief. In Luke 8, Jesus allowed only Peter, James, and John to enter with Him and commanded mockers to leave. He allowed Jairus to stay, who had demonstrated faith by seeking Jesus out in the first place. Jesus told Jairus not to be afraid, to trust. Scripture says Jairus was absolutely overwhelmed by the miracle of his daughter's resurrection.

30) Personal answer. A person might feel shame when asking for prayer if their sickness relates to private areas of the body or mind. They may feel shame because they believe sickness is their fault or they are sick because they aren't holy enough. They may feel they are at fault for lack of faith. They may have been told they are sick because of hidden sin (though most people I have encountered with this problem have no clue what the "hidden sin" is and torment themselves to remember it). They may have asked for prayer once and been told that once they have been prayed for the sickness is healed, no matter how they feel, and it is wrong to ask again. There are many reasons why people may be ashamed to ask for prayer.

31) Personal observation.
Jesus took a blind man outside of his "village" (I read mentality and perhaps a certain atmosphere) and healed him.

32) Personal observation.
When the blind man said he was not totally healed, Jesus prayed again.

33) Personal answer.
When a person has not manifested total healing, I would pray again.

34) Personal answer.
I would hope to flow freely with the Holy Spirit into each situation. I would listen to the person and then listen to what the Spirit has to say. In the first instance, my thought was to serve, not judge. The Hindu lady was truthful and the Spirit did a beautiful work. In the second instance, God uncovered the deception. These two experiences remind me not to put too much emphasis on what a person says, but trust the Holy Spirit to glorify Jesus Christ.

35) Personal answer.
The Holy Spirit counsels me to believe, to trust, and to seek understanding. I know I must pray for discernment to move wisely and encourage others to reach out for healing through Jesus Christ for every circumstance.

ANSWER KEY

PART THREE
LESSON FOUR

GREATER THINGS

GREATER THINGS

1) Scripture shows Jesus calling people to repentance. The Word records Jesus healing the sick, delivering the demonized, encouraging His disciples to desire more, and teaching through stories. I notice Jesus talks with the general crowd, then takes time to share the deeper meaning of His teachings with His disciples. Jesus eats with people who are despised by the "religious", lays His life down for His friends, and raises the dead.

2) Greater things means Jesus is going to do more than what I've read about in the gospels. I expect a supernatural "more". I expect to be part of the "greater things".

3) I've seen extraordinary results for myself and others when, through the power of the Holy Spirit, I've forgiven as the gospels tell me Jesus forgave.

4) Body ministry is broad in scope. I have given many examples, but I just received a phone call reminding me of another aspect of Body ministry.   I've just spoken with Carl and Denise, a husband and wife who had invited me to their home to minister to friends. Carl said, "The people who came knew they were at more than a prayer meeting when you prayed with them. You ministered to their needs. We know them all, and you spoke to each one right where their lives were at." Those who had gathered prayed over me at the end of our meeting. They spoke encouragement into my life, prophetic word I knew was true, and released Holy Spirit power for me. They spoke to me of things they did not know, but I knew. The Body ministered to each other that day. Each one gave and received as inspired by the Spirit.

5) Bridge for Peace has undertaken many Spirit-led projects that could not have been accomplished by any one individual. The King of Christmas event required over 60 volunteers, plus dozens of worship leaders. Hundreds of people heard the gospel preached! A Bridge for Peace mission team mounted a great effort called Heart Spa, ministering to women in Mississippi after the Katrina disaster and at another time to women from Long Island, NY. It took Spirit, heart, strength, and lots of coordination to deliver the blessings!   Our Body ministry events are too many to count!

6) I remember when I didn't have any role models for the way I was called to follow Him. When I found one in a book, a huge obstacle was removed. I still seek role models in men and women willing to follow God however He calls.

7) Filling up on the Holy Spirit through prayer and the Word definitely moves me forward through all obstacles. My plan for receiving what I need is to set aside time for daily fellowship with Him and leave space for God to move me in His creative ways.

8) Perseverance is holy and necessary for me to see God's greater things. It's a continual going forward despite obstacles.

9) When persevering in prayer I have felt many things, including the sense of God's pleasure. I've also felt a desire to quit, a sense of great hope, and other contradictory emotions. Whatever our feelings, we know the Holy Spirit gives us the power to persevere.

10) Yes, I can give plenty of examples of perseverance. Finishing this Course after two years is the latest example! And finishing the Course in our new house built by God's Word after persevering for twenty years is a double blessing. In both situations I have been helped by the people God has put around me.

11) When I'm persevering I know I'm leaning on God's power and I thank Him for it. When I'm striving, I forget His Presence.

12) The time to discern whether or not to begin, is before beginning. I like to have a Word from God on a project. If God gives me a Word, a vision, or another sense of His will, I refer to it as I work the project through. If it gets difficult I might wonder, *"How did I get into this?"* Then I have a clear, encouraging answer, if I have begun well. If I didn't begin well, and the project was not of God, then it is time to repent and scrap the project. If it was of God, but I began badly, it's time to repent and make a new beginning asking Him to be the Head of the work.

13) I can tell if I get off track by striving, because the feeling around the work is totally different. The sense of pressure is different. Paying attention to my feelings and attitudes around the work helps me to notice if I'm striving or persevering.

14) I have prayed for many things that have taken awhile to manifest. While not easy, I have learned precious lessons through waiting. I am still persevering in prayer for unresolved situations and I'm still learning.

15) Jesus showed me He sometimes had to pray twice and He was willing to pray twice. I think I should follow the same pattern.

16) Yes. I have sometimes thought I was overcoming a large obstacle, but realize now I wasn't even in Holy Spirit nursery school. I have sometimes thought it was time for me to move on to the next lesson, when God's plan still called for years of training me in that same lesson.

17) I sense a definite connection between perseverance and greater things. I think of the many years we waited for the Brazil mission. None of us could have possibly been ready for it a moment earlier. He prepared us as we persevered and we saw the greater things in group deliverance and cancerous tumors vanishing. Who knows what God is preparing us for right now as we persevere?

18) Personal answer.
The Blood Covenant Prayer rejuvenates me. Thank you, Jesus Christ, Father, and Holy Spirit for giving me Your Word and allowing me to receive Your promises.

NOW AVAILABLE!

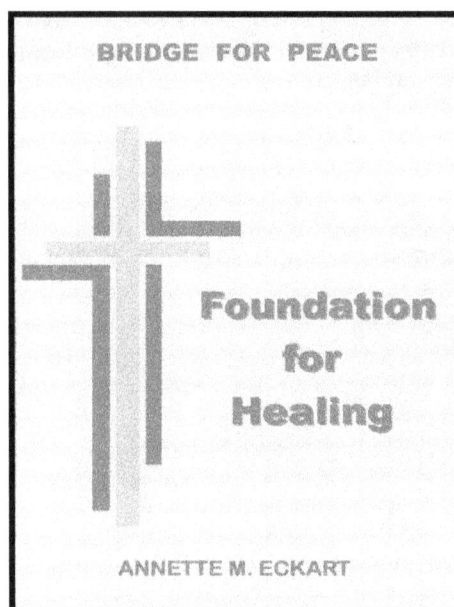

BRIDGE FOR PEACE

Foundation
for
Healing

ANNETTE M. ECKART

Companion DVD for use with the *Foundation for Healing Course*

12 exciting teachings on 2 discs covering the Blood, Authority, Holy Spirit Empowerment, and more!

These teachings lay a strong foundation for anyone seeking to be healed or to launch out into healing ministry. They are designed in 20 minute segments for prayer groups or individual study.

Call (631) 730-3982 now
Or visit www.bridgeforpeace.org

www.ingramcontent.com/pod-product-compliance
Lightning Source LLC
Chambersburg PA
CBHW062102090426

42741CB00015B/3306